HELLO WORLD
THE MANGA

MANGA BY MANATSU SUZUKI AND YOSHIHIRO SONO
ORIGINAL CONCEPT: "HELLO WORLD" PRODUCTION COMMITTEE

CONTENTS

KATAGAKI NAOMI.
Phase1
I'M YOU, TEN YEARS FROM NOW.
FZZ FZZ...

AND I'M HERE TO GRANT YOUR WISH.
Phase 1

2027, Kyoto.
SPRING IS THE SEASON OF NEW BEGINNINGS, OR SO I'VE HEARD.

MAYBE IT'S THAT TIME OF YEAR OR SOMETHING, BUT I JUST WISH...
The One
THAT SOMETHING AMAZING, LIKE YOU'D FIND IN A NOVEL, WOULD HAPPEN.
BLINK BLINK
The One

UH!
ERM...
OH NO!
DASH
SAFE!
PLINK

BUT EVEN IF SOMETHING AMAZING HAPPENED...

I PROBABLY WOULDN'T DO ANYTHING.

I JUST WATCH OTHER PEOPLE HAVE ADVENTURES.

I'M AN EXTRA.

HEY, YOU'RE KATAGAKI-KUN, RIGHT?

WE'RE ALL HANGING OUT AFTER CLASS.
WE MIGHT GO TO KARAOKE.
WANNA COME, KATAGAKI-KUN?
WHAT?

UH!

SING IN FRONT OF EVERY-ONE?

BUT SHE DID BOTHER TO INVITE ME...
OH!

IT'S OKAY IF YOU'RE BUSY.
WHAT?

OH... NO...

SORRY TO BUG YOU!
HEY, HURRY UP! LET'S GO!

WAIT!
THE KARAOKE PLACE IN KAWARA-MACHI?

IT'S ALWAYS LIKE THIS.

I'M SUPER INDECISIVE.

I HATE BEING SO TIMID.
STARTING HIGH SCHOOL WAS SUPPOSED TO BE A FRESH START FOR ME, BUT...
NOTHING'S CHANGED AT ALL.

NO.
ENOUGH!
CLATTER
I CAN'T STAY THIS WAY!
OOGAKI BOOKS
OOGAKI BOOKS

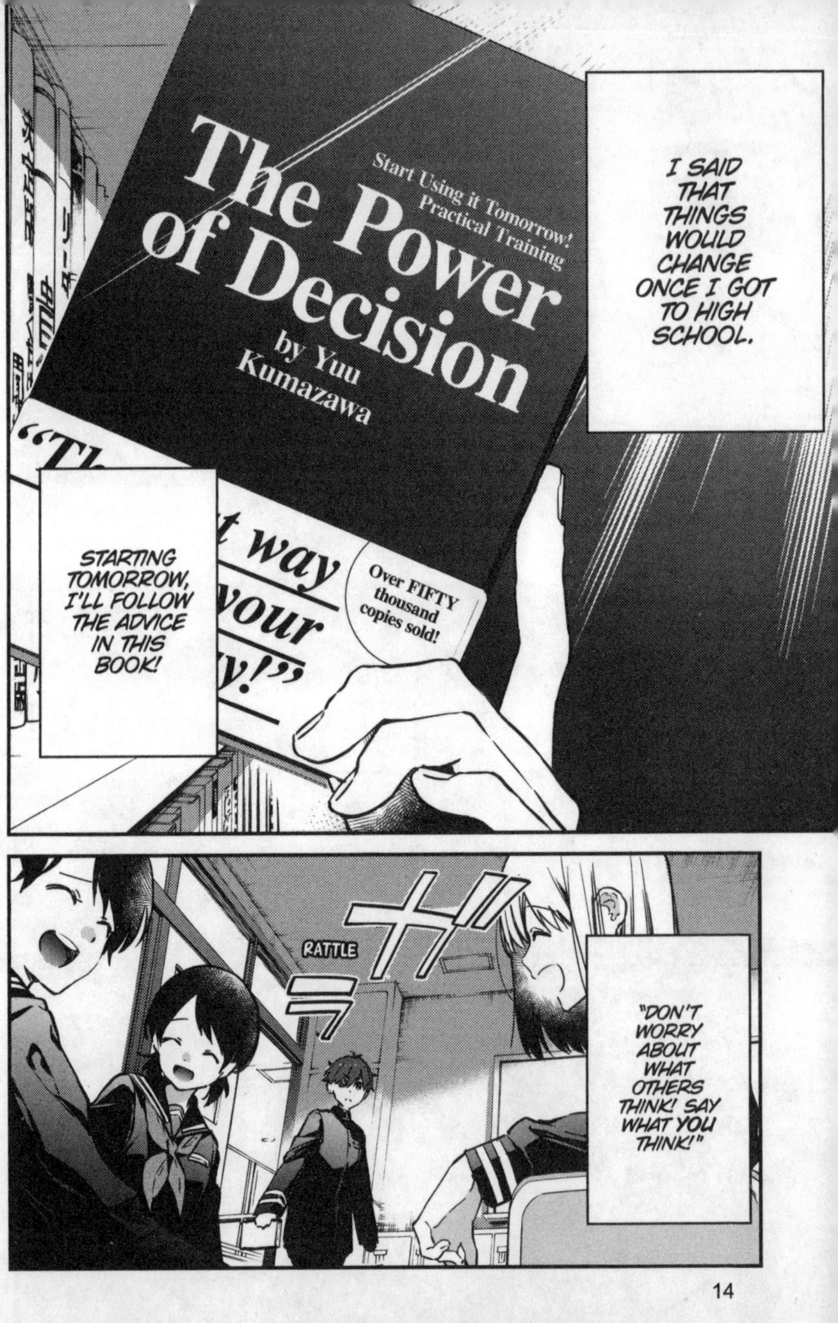

I SAID THAT THINGS WOULD CHANGE ONCE I GOT TO HIGH SCHOOL.

The Power of Decision

Start Using it Tomorrow! Practical Training

by Yuu Kumazawa

Over FIFTY thousand copies sold!

STARTING TOMORROW, I'LL FOLLOW THE ADVICE IN THIS BOOK!

UH! THAT'S...
AH HA HA.
MY SEAT...
......
IT'S FUNNY THOUGH
SERIOUSLY?
AND THEN...
AH HA HA HA!
THEY'RE HAVING SO MUCH FUN. I SHOULDN'T INTERRUPT THEM, RIGHT?
YEAH.
FLUTTER
OOGAKI BOOKS
IT'S NOT LIKE I *HAVE* TO SIT THERE RIGHT NOW OR ANYTHING, AND...

SEAT. MOVE.

OH, I'M SORRY.

WE'LL GO OVER THERE.

CLATTER

CLATTER

......

WOW!

YAKI-
NIKU...
NO,
FISH.

FISH
SANDWICH,
PLEASE.
SAME
HERE!

!

Yakiniku Roll
Fish Sandwich

THEN,
I'LL GO
WITH A
YAKINIKU
ROLL...
うおおお!
WHOOOOA!
おおお
OOOH!

Yakiniku Roll
Fish Sandwich

NEJIRI-
PAN'S
OKAY.
GOT
IT.

NEJIRI-
PAN,
PLEASE.

HERE
YA GO.

"DON'T LET OTHERS DECIDE FOR YOU. THINK FOR YOURSELF!"
KATAGAKI, YOU CAN BE THE LIBRARY AIDE BECAUSE YOU LIKE BOOKS, OKAY?
EH?!
O-OKAY.
GOOD. IT'S DECIDED THEN.
ずぅぅぅん
DEPRESSED
I'M COMPLETELY FAILING AT ASSERTING MYSELF!!!
IT'S LIKE I HAVE NO AGENCY AT ALL!
WELL, I WAS THINKING IT WOULDN'T BE SO BAD TO BE A LIBRARY AIDE.
I GUESS IT'S OKAY.
NOW, FROM THE GIRLS...

THAT BLUNT GIRL FROM EARLIER...

UGH.

I HAVE TO BE AN AIDE WITH HER?

Today: Library Aide Meeting

REALLY? I LIVED AROUND THERE IN JUNIOR HIGH!

H-HEY.

Blush

Organizing Bookshel

Rotation

How to use POS

Charity Used Book Sale at about the end of June

OKAY, LET'S HAVE A GREAT YEAR, EVERY-ONE!

THAT'S ALL.

KADENO-KOUJI-SAN, LET'S EXCHANGE INFO!
OKAY.
ME TOO!
AND ME!
......
UHH...
WELL, IT'S ENOUGH TO BE IN THE SAME GROUP AS KADENOKOUJI-SAN...
HMM?
WHO'S THIS UNLISTED ACCOUNT?
no name
You
Takeshi

STOMP
スタ
STOMP
スタ
STOMP
スタ
FLINCH
びくっ

EEK!
RUMMAGE
RUMMAGE

...?
SHE'S NOT USED TO USING A SMART PHONE...?
POKE

DO YOU HAVE THE APP ON YOUR PHONE?
TAP TAP TAP
TAP TAP

YOU DON'T KNOW YOUR PHONE NUMBER...?

YANK
RUSTLE RUSTLE
SHING

Scribble scribble scribble
RIP

WHAP

...
HER AD-DRESS?
606 0831 Sakyo-ku
Shimogamo Kibunecho 40
Ichigyou Ruri

IF YOU NEED ANYTHING, CONTACT ME WITH THAT.

ALL RIGHT.

NOTHING WENT LIKE THE BOOK SAID IT WOULD.

DOES ICHIGYOU-SAN HATE ME?

BUT IT'S NOT LIKE I DID ANYTHING WRONG, RIGHT?
I WONDER WHAT I SHOULD'VE DONE?

IF I WAS A PROTA-GONIST...

I COULD DECIDE LOTS OF STUFF REALLY FAST!

I'D GET ALONG WITH EVERY-ONE!

AND...

THE CUTE HEROINE WOULD...

IF I COULD CHANGE JUST THE TINIEST BIT, THEN...

MAYBE I COULD ENJOY HIGH SCHOOL?

I'M NOT ASKING FOR MUCH. I DON'T WANT TO SEEM GREEDY OR TEMPT FATE.

BUT...

The One
WHAT'S GOING ON...?
AN AURORA ...?
IN JAPAN?

TWAK

HUNH.
A CROW?
ITS LEGS...
CHOMP
EEK!
CAW!
FWIP
PLOP
WAIT A MINUTE!
OH!
FLAP
FLAP

OOGAKI BOOKS

Huff!
Huff!
Huff!
Huff!

Flap
FWIP
Tunk

SERI-OUSLY, BIRD?

I RAN ALL THE WAY TO FUSHIMI INARI.

I HAVEN'T COME OUT HERE IN A WHILE.

SHIVER

WHAT?

SOME-THING'S WRONG.

THERE ARE USUALLY MORE TOURISTS HERE, BUT...
ZRRR
ZRR
ZRR

KIIIIN
WHAT?
ZRR
ZRR
ZRR

WHA ...?
WHAT WAS THAT?
WHOA!!
KIIIIN

GWOO
WHOAAA!
WHAAAT?!
WHOA!!
HE'S GOING TO LAND ON ME!

SWOO
WHAT?
CRASH

OOF!
Huff!
Huff!
Huff!
GRIP
GRIP
I'M IN?
I DID IT!

I MADE IT!!

GOOD.

IT WORKED!

MUMBLE

MUMBLE

WHAT'S WITH HIM?

HE PHASED RIGHT THROUGH ME!

EEK...

YOU KNOW WHAT? NONE OF MY BUSINESS! I'LL JUST GO...

PANIC

PANIC

BECAUSE...
I'M YOU, TEN YEARS FROM NOW.

AND I'M HERE TO GRANT YOUR WISH.

ME...

TEN YEARS FROM NOW?

IT'S HERE.

THAT SOMETHING AMAZING, LIKE YOU'D FIND IN A NOVEL...

IT'S HAPPENING!

YOU...

WANT A GIRL-FRIEND.

NO, NOT REALLY--
HOLD IT *RIGHT* THERE.

NO. REALLY.
THREE MONTHS FROM TODAY...

YOU'LL HAVE A GIRL-FRIEND!

WHAT?!

A GIRL CALLED ICHIGYOU RURI.
RUSTLE
RUSTLE
WHAAAAT?!

HELLO WORLD
THE MANGA

Phase2

SOMEONE WHO CLAIMED TO BE ME TEN YEARS FROM NOW APPEARED, AND...

SAID I'D HAVE A GIRLFRIEND IN THREE MONTHS.

...!
Plop

SORRY...

Flip

I'M SUP-
POSED
TO BE...

Phase2
ICHIGYOU RURI-SAN'S...
BOY-FRIEND.

Yesterday.

UMM...

......

WHERE'RE YOU GOING?

DRONES OUT TODAY, TOO, HUH?

Whirr

WELL, OF COURSE THEY'RE FLYING!

OH!

whisper whisper

DON'T CAUSE A SCENE.

NO ONE ELSE CAN SEE ME. ONLY YOU.

......
THAT'S RIGHT.

IT DOES SEEM LIKE ONLY I SEE HIM...
AND HEAR HIM, TOO.

HE DOESN'T REALLY LOOK LIKE ME.
IS HE REALLY ME FROM THE FUTURE?
IS HE JUST A DELUSION?
OR MAYBE A HALLUCI-NATION?
YOU KNOW ABOUT "CHRONICLE KYOTO," RIGHT?
...
HUH?

UH...
WELL, YES.
CHRONI-CLE KYOTO...
IS A PROJECT INTENDED TO BE PART R&D, PART MAP SERVICE.
THE GOAL IS TO RECORD KYOTO IN A MUCH MORE DETAILED AND ACCURATE WAY.
BY PURSUING CHANGES IN TIME SHIFTS...
THEY'RE TRYING TO RECORD INFORMATION FROM VARIOUS TIME PERIODS.
pluura
THE REQUIRED MEMORY WAS MADE POSSIBLE...
WITH THE WORLD'S LARGEST WEB SERVICE COMPANY, PLUURA, AND THEIR QUANTUM COMPUTER TECH.

WITH THE HELP FROM KYOTO COLLEGE'S PROFESSOR SENKO, THE QUANTUM MEMORY APPARATUS WAS BUILT.

THE "ALLTALE."

ALLTALE

THE ALLTALE'S MEMORY IS MANY TIMES GREATER THAN MOST COMPUTERS.
IT'S HUNDREDS OF MILLIONS... *TRILLIONS* MORE.
HELL, THE ALLTALE'S MEMORY IS INFINITE.

......
OH. WOW.

BUT WHAT DOES THAT HAVE TO DO WITH YOU AND ME?

RUN!
WE DON'T HAVE TIME!
WHAT?
DASH

HEY--!
WAAAAIT!
DASH DASH
DASH

MADE IT.
Huff!
Huff!
WHERE ARE WE?
THIS IS THE MIDDLE OF NOWHERE!
NO, THERE IS SOME-THING HERE.
IN 2020, THE TRUE INITIATIVE FOR CHRONICLE KYOTO WAS SECRETLY LAUNCHED.
A RECORDED EVENT.

IT'S NOT ONLY THAT THEY'RE RECORDING KYOTO WITH A LOT OF RECORDING MACHINERY.

THAT INITIATIVE COVERS *EVERYTHING* ABOUT KYOTO.
THE TOWN, PEOPLE, EVENTS.
ANYTHING AND EVERYTHING THAT HAPPENS IN KYOTO, THE ALLTALE WILL RECORD IT ALL.
ALLTALE

......
ALL...?

Whirrr

!

KATAGAKI NAOMI WAS READING A BOOK BY THE RIVERSIDE, WHEN...

HE WAS INJURED BY A FALLING DRONE.

THAT'S WHAT WAS RECORDED.

RE-CORD-ED?

THAT'S RIGHT.

THIS IS THE KYOTO OF THE PAST, AS RECORDED BY ALLTALE.

KATAGAKI NAOMI OF THE PAST...

AS RECORDED BY THE ALLTALE.

……
THAT MEANS …
THAT GUY'S NOT JUST A TIME TRAVELER.

HE'S ME IN TEN YEARS, WHO'S LOGGED INTO...
THE WORLD FROM TEN YEARS AGO ON THE QUANTUM COMPUTER, ALLTALE.

THAT MEANS THIS WORLD...
AND EVERYTHING IN IT HAS ALREADY BEEN RECORDED.

I'M JUST A BIT OF DATA IN THERE. THAT'S ALL.

......
AND...

THE REASON HE'S COME...

Hover...

GRRRR
RRR...
??
?

GRRRR...
?

IS TO GET ME A GIRL-FRIEND?!

ERM!

SERI-OUSLY?!

THUNK
ゴッ
OW!

OH.
FLAP
FLAP

TILT
HUH?
WHAT NOW?
HEY!
WHOOSH
ばっ
WAIT!
WAIT!
TAK TAK TAK
dash
ばた
dash
ばた
てててて—
TAK TAK TAK TAK
OH...

SHH.

PHASE

YOU CAN "TALK TO YOURSELF" HERE, RIGHT?
JAB JAB
RIGHT. THANKS FOR THAT, I GUESS.

SO.
NOW THAT YOU'VE SLEPT ON IT, WHAT DO YOU THINK?

OKAY. I GUESS.
GOOD.
BUT...
THERE'S *NO WAY* I'M GOING TO DATE ICHIGYOU-SAN IN THREE MONTHS!
......
SO YOU CAN BELIEVE THAT THIS IS A DIGITAL WORLD...
BUT *THAT'S* THE PART THAT'S TOO MUCH FOR YOU?!
WELL, YEAH!

順列都市
PERMUTATION CITY
I READ A LOT OF SCI-FI.
LIKE GREG EGAN AND STUFF.

......
IF I'M JUST DATA...
THEN I CAN'T EXPERIENCE THE REAL WORLD...

OR TELL ONE WORLD FROM ANOTHER.
SO HOW AM I SUPPOSED TO VERIFY YOUR STORY?

RIGHT?

......
YOU...

NO, I WAS DEFINITELY LIKE THAT.

I CAN BELIEVE THAT YOU'RE TELLING THE TRUTH.
KIND OF.
BUT...
BUT?

HONESTLY, I LIKE CUTE, BUBBLY GIRLS.

ICHIGYOU-SAN LOOKS LIKE SHE'D KILL YOU JUST FOR COMING TOO CLOSE.

GLOOOM

THAT KIND OF GIRL, WELL...

MAYBE YOU'RE THINKING OF THE WRONG PERSON!
I'M GOING TO FIND OUT!
H-HANG ON...
SEE, THAT'S ICHIGYOU-SAN.
WE'RE BOTH LIBRARY AIDES SO IT'S NOT LIKE I COULD MISTAKE HER FOR SOMEONE ELSE.

LIGHTNING STRUCK A TREE AT THE FIREWORKS FESTIVAL.
SHE WAS *RIGHT* NEXT TO IT.

RIGHT AFTER WE STARTED DATING...

SHE NEVER OPENED HER EYES AGAIN.

WHAT?

MY GOAL IS TO CHANGE THE RECORD.

...

I'LL PREVENT THE INCIDENT FROM HAPPEN-ING.

THEN SHE WON'T DIE, AND...

IT'LL BE THE CATALYST FOR CHANGE. THE RECORDS WILL BE REWRITTEN.

INSIDE THAT INFINITE MEMORY, A WORLD WHERE ICHIGYOU RURI LIVES WILL EXIST.

SHE WON'T COME BACK.

THEN *WHY*...?

WE DIDN'T GO ANYWHERE TOGETHER.

WE DON'T HAVE ANY MEMORIES TOGETHER.

WE DON'T EVEN HAVE ONE PICTURE OF US.

JUST ONCE IS ENOUGH.

I JUST WANT HER SMILING AND HAPPY.
EVEN IF IT ISN'T REAL.
EVEN IF...
SHE'S NOT SMILING AT ME.

LEND ME A HAND?
EH?
BUT...
TMP
SHFF
I CAN'T DO ANY-THING.
I'M JUST AN AVATAR, SO I CAN'T PHYSICALLY INTERACT WITH THIS WORLD.

I'M POWERLESS.
PLEASE.
LEND ME YOUR STRENGTH.

IF THERE'S...

SOMETHING I CAN DO, THEN...

WHAT SHOULD I CALL YOU?

?

I MEAN, LIKE YOU'RE ME AND EVERYTHING, SO...

CALL ME SENSEI.

AFTER ALL, I'M TEN YEARS YOUR SENIOR AND I'M GOING TO TEACH YOU LOTS!

YOU'RE NO LONGER POWERLESS.

NOW YOU HAVE ME, AND...

?

FLOAT

!

FLAP

FLAP

MY BUDDY HERE, TOO.

WHOOOSH
WHA...
FLASH
WITH MY BUDDY...
YOU CAN BECOME THE GOD OF THIS MEMORY.

HELLO WORLD
THE MANGA

Phase3

IMAGINE SOMETHING THAT'S ALWAYS AROUND YOU.

PICTURE IT AS CLEARLY AS YOU CAN.

PLASTIC.

RUBBER.

PAPER.

FOCUS AND...

GRAB IT!

FLASH

WHOA!!

THIS IS THE GOD HAND!

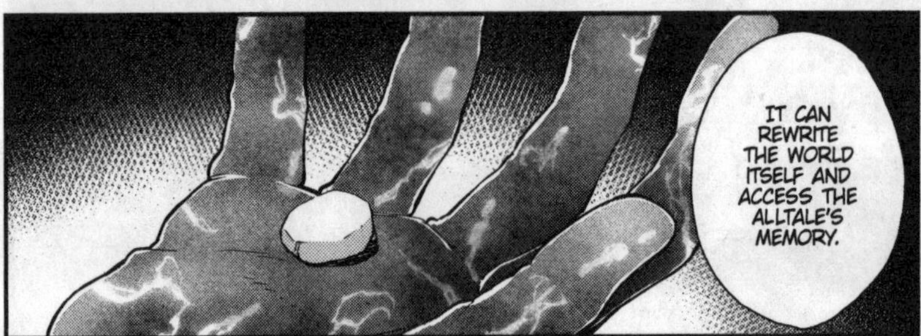
IT CAN REWRITE THE WORLD ITSELF AND ACCESS THE ALLTALE'S MEMORY.

ROLL
DIRT CLOD TO JEWEL.

SPLASH
AIR TO WATER.

STOP

BLIP

NOTHING TO SOMETHING.

BYUU

WHA!

I CAN ONLY MAKE ILLUSIONS.

SINCE I'M AN AVATAR, I DON'T HAVE MANY RIGHTS WITHIN ALLTALE.

BUT BECAUSE THE GOD HAND HAS PHYSICAL RIGHTS...

IT CAN TOUCH AND MANIPULATE THINGS.

GYUU
IN THEORY, BUT THERE ARE A LOT OF RESTRICTIONS.

I CAN DO...
ANYTHING?

THAT MEANS...

FIRST OFF, YOU CAN ONLY CHANGE AS MUCH DATA AS THE GLOVE CAN TOUCH.
Direct touch.
In the air's okay, too.
Far away is no good.
YOU CAN'T MAKE THINGS AND STUFF FROM A DISTANCE.

ALSO, PROCESSING SPEED DEPENDS ON THE AMOUNT OF DATA.
WATER AND INORGANIC SUBSTANCES ARE EASY, BUT TRYING TO MAKE A LIVING ORGANISM GROW IS REALLY HARD.

ESPECIALLY THINGS LIKE A BRAIN-- THE HUMAN CONSCIOUSNESS IS LIKE THE ULTIMATE IN DATA DENSITY.
YOU WON'T BE ABLE TO CHANGE IT, EVEN WITH THE GOD HAND.

THAT MEANS I CAN'T MAKE ICHIGYOU-SAN LIKE ME, THEN.

THAT'S...

MY JOB!
LogicalAir
Ultimate Manual

Vroom...

APRIL 20TH.
I RODE THE BUS, HEADED FOR THE NORTH LIBRARY.
RATTLE
RATTLE
LogicalAir

THEN AT THAT MOMENT...
IT HAPPENED. THE EVENT THAT CLOSED THE GAP BETWEEN US.

YOU JUST HAVE TO DO WHAT'S WRITTEN DOWN ABOUT THE FUTURE IN *THIS.*

LogicalAir

Ultimate Manual

WHAT SHOULD I DO, SENSEI?!

FIRST, TAKE OUT THE BOOK.
COUGH COUGH
OOPS.
OH.
OPEN IT.

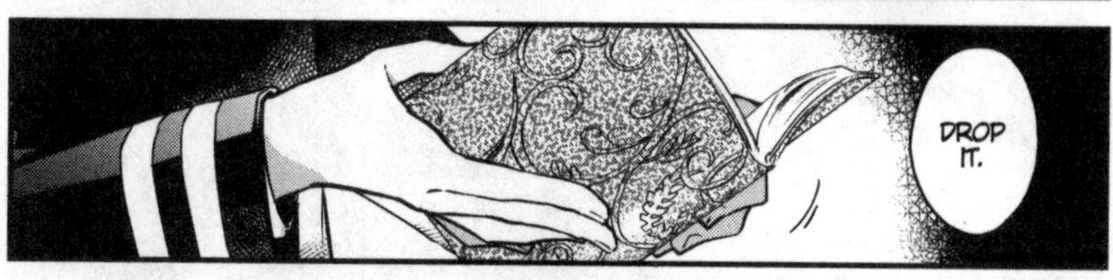
DROP IT.

TA-TUNK

CLANK
RATTLE RATTLE

UMM?
PICK IT UP.

......
RATTLE
LURCH
WHAT IS THIS...?

SQUISH
!
ガタン
CLANK

EEK!
GLARE
GLAAAARE

WHAP
STMP
STMP

OKAY!
THROB THROB

IT IS NOT OKAY! SHE OBVIOUSLY HATES ME NOW!
HOW IS THAT AN ULTIMATE MANUAL?!
CALM DOWN.

!

UH!
UM...

STARE

UNGH...

ABOUT YESTERDAY... I'M SORRY...

I DROPPED MY BOOK AND WHEN I WENT TO PICK IT UP...

……

I'VE BEEN LOOKING FOR THAT.

CLATTER

SORRY FOR JUMPING TO CON-CLUSIONS.

BOW

THANK YOU.
STMP
STMP
SO MAYBE WE *DID* GROW A LITTLE BIT CLOSER...
VRZZ VRZZ VRZZ

A LITTLE BIT.

DON'T SWEAT IT.

THIS RELATION-SHIP'S JUST STARTING.

VRZZ
VRZZ
VRZZ

WIZ Library Aides Group
President
Monday Bookshelf Cleaning
Everyone, please bring your own dust cloths.
Please make sure to pass this along on Saturday.
DUST CLOTHS, HUH?

PASS THIS ALONG? BUT ICHIGYOU-SAN'S NOT IN THE GROUP CHAT AND I DON'T KNOW HER PHONE NUMBER, EITHER.

USE THIS.

?

AN ENVELOPE?

Ichigyou Ruri

Today
Library
Aide
Meeting
THEN, WE'LL MOVE ON TO CLEANING.
PLEASE USE YOUR OWN DUST CLOTHS.

IT LOOKS LIKE SHE GOT MY LETTER, BUT...

SHE'S NOT TREATING ME ANY DIFFER-ENTLY.

TO BE HONEST, IT'S STILL SCARY TALKING TO HER.

Thank you for letting me know.

ICHIGYOU-SAN WROTE THAT POLITE REPLY WITH SUCH A STONY FACE.

AH HA HA HA HA HA!

IT WAS STRANGE AND KIND OF FUNNY.

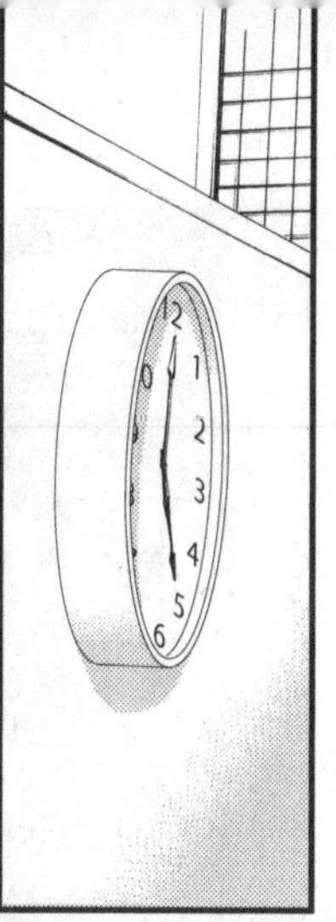

SHALL WE GO CLOSE UP?

WELL, SEE YOU LATER.
?

WE WERE ON THE SAME BUS BEFORE, SO PERHAPS WE LIVE NEAR EACH OTHER?

UH... NO...
IT'S JUST... WHEN I...

...

I WAS AT THE LIBRARY THAT DAY AND...

THAT'S THE ONLY PLACE AROUND HERE THAT HAS *DEDUCTION MAGAZINE*, SO...
......

I SEE.
Phssssh

I...

READ IT THERE EVERY MONTH, AS WELL.
TAP
TAP

PHSSSH

VROOM
VROOOO...

DID SHE...
JUST SMILE?

WOW!
RUSTLE RUSTLE

RUSTLE
IT WENT JUST LIKE SENSEI SAID!

THE MANUAL'S AMAZING!
IT'S GOT WHAT WILL HAPPEN AND WHAT I NEED TO DO!
Ichigyou-san will ask about the bus. Going home a differe way? Goal? Suspicious? Good way to change the subject: Bring up the subject of the magazine at the library?
AS LONG AS I DO WHAT IT SAYS, EVEN THINGS THAT SEEM IMPOSSIBLE WILL WORK OUT.

THE RESULTS ARE GUARANTEED, SO...

BWOOSH

SENSEI, LOOK! IT'S IRON! IRON!
TROT TROT TROT

WHOOOOSH
!
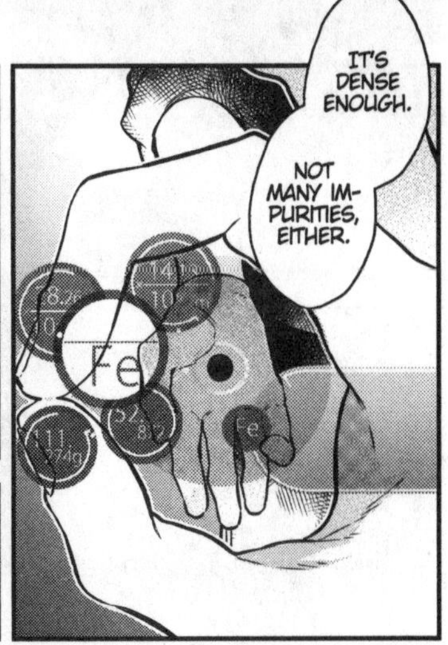
IT'S DENSE ENOUGH.
NOT MANY IMPURITIES, EITHER.
Fe

ISN'T THIS AMAZING?!
I'VE BEEN PRACTICING!
HEH HEH!

WHOA!
THUD
THUD
THUD
THUD
THUD
THUD

IT'S AN IMAGE.
HUH?
DON'T BE AFRAID. DO SOMETHING.

NO WAY! IT'S IMPOSSIBLE!
IMPOSSIBLE?

ARE YOU GOING TO SAY THAT WHEN THE TIME COMES, TOO?
THE GOD HAND HAS THE POWER TO AVERT THE ACCIDENT...
BUT IT'S UP TO YOU TO USE IT TO DEFEND HER.
YOU BETTER GET GOING OR YOU'LL BE LATE.
OH, WAIT!

IT'S TODAY.
......
CREAK...

SPIN
SWAY
OH...
UGH...
THUNK
OOF!

I KNEW THIS'D HAPPEN BUT...

I COULDN'T SAVE HER AT ALL.

FROM NOW ON, I'LL DO THE HIGH SHELVES OF THE BOOK-CASES.
THEN I'LL DO THE LOWER SHELVES.
NO, I'LL DO THOSE, TOO!
THE LARGE FORMAT BOOKS ON THE BOTTOM SHELVES ARE HEAVY, SO...
THE MIDDLE SHELVES THEN?
THAT WORKS.
THANK YOU...
KATAGAKI-SAN.

DIVIDING THE SHELVES INTO TOP, MIDDLE, AND BOTTOM WAS REALLY INEFFECTIVE.

THAT'S NICE.
YOU EXCHANGED INFO WITH A GIRL FOR THE FIRST TIME.

WHAT? WELL...
EH HEH HEH!

HELLO WORLD
THE MANGA

Phase 4
WE NEED TO COLLECT BOOKS FOR THE USED BOOK SALE ON JUNE 25TH.
SO, WE'LL PLACE A BOX OUTSIDE OF THIS LIBRARY AND EVERY CLASS-ROOM STARTING TOMORROW.
June 25th Charity Used Book Sale
THEN OTHER STUDENTS CAN DONATE BOOKS.

WE'LL NEED SOME-ONE TO MAN THE STORE, HUH?
RATTLE RATTLE
RATTLE
OH!
SHOPGIRLS USUALLY WEAR CUTE CLOTHES, RIGHT?
SHOP-GIRLS...
CUTE CLOTH-ES, LIKE...
COS-PLAY?
NYAN...
JOLT
?
RUFFLE RUFFLE

SO, WE'RE GOING TO SET UP THIS DONATION BOX.
WE APPRECIATE YOUR CO-OPERATION.
DONATIONS
THIS IS IT, HUH?

THE USED BOOK SALE IN JUNE IS A BIG EVENT FOR US.
COLLECT A LOT OF BOOKS AND CLOSE THE GAP BETWEEN YOU.
UNDER-STOOD!
GOLD.
NNGH!
GRIT...
RAAAAR

DONATIONS

I GUESS THIS IS HOW IT GOES, RIGHT?

NO.

ONCE WE'VE DECIDED TO COLLECT THEM, WE **MUST** DO THE BEST WE CAN.

LET'S GET THIS DONE!

June 25th
Charity Used Book Sale
3 Days Left
Current Count
37 books

DO THE BEST YOU CAN!
IF YOU HAVE SOME AT HOME, BRING THEM IN.

MY LATE GRAND-FATHER COLLECTED BOOKS.

I WONDERED IF ONE PERSON SHOULD BRING IN SO MANY BUT...

LET'S DONATE SOME OF THESE.

......
WOW.

ARE YOU *SURE?*
AREN'T THEY YOUR GRAND-FATHER'S--WELL *YOUR*--PRECIOUS BOOKS, ICHIGYOU-SAN?

OF COURSE, I FEEL WEIRD ABOUT SOMEONE ELSE BUYING THEM...
Paff
Paff
BUT A BOOK WANTS TO BE READ, CORRECT?

......
THEN...
LET'S BRING THEM IN.

BUT HOW?

HUFF!
WE CAN CARRY THEM.
HUFF!
HUFF!
IT'D COST MONEY TO HAVE THEM DELIVERED, SO...

KAWAMITSU WATER
Gulp
Gulp

SIGH...

......
CRUNCH
CRUNCH
CRUNCH

KATAGAKI-SAN, WHAT KIND OF BOOKS DO YOU LIKE?
WHAT?

I SEE.

......!

I'M HOPELESS.

WITHOUT THE MANUAL TO GO BY, I'M LOST.

THAT WAS THE BEST I COULD COME UP WITH?!

I...

LIKE ADVENTURE NOVELS.
TAKING ON CHALLEN-GES...
AND SEEING THEM THROUGH TO THE END WITHOUT QUITTING. IT'S INSPIRING.
I WANT TO LIVE...
LIKE THAT.
ICHIGYOU-SAN'S TALKING ABOUT HER-SELF...
AND HER FEELINGS?
THAT'S A FIRST.

BUT I...!
UH!
I...

I LIKE SCI-FI.

IT SHOWS ME AMAZING NEW WORLDS.
BUT THEY AREN'T LIKE DREAMS OR FANTASY WORLDS. THEY'RE AN EXTENSION OF REALITY.

IT FEELS LIKE *I'M* A PART OF THE STORY.

WHAT IN THE WORLD AM I SAYING?
THE REAL ME'S JUST LIKE AN EXTRA OR SOMETHING, THOUGH.
I CAN'T EXPLAIN IT WELL...

BUT I LOVE SCI-FI...!
I SEE.
WHAT'S WITH ME?
I CAN'T DO ANYTHING UNLESS IT'S BY THE MANUAL.
I CAN'T EVEN TALK ABOUT MYSELF WITHOUT LOOKING LIKE A DORK.
AT THIS RATE...
THAT FEELING...

I FEEL THAT WAY SOMETIMES, TOO.
SHAA

OH!
THIS BOOK...
The City at the Bottom of the Big Lake
I KIND OF WANT TO READ IT.

THEN WHY DON'T YOU TAKE IT?
I'LL BUY IT AT THE BOOK SALE.
HM?

A BOOK CARD...
Title The City at the Bottom of the Big Lake
Date Loaned
Borrower's Name
Date Due
Date Returned
7 6 Ogiwara Yumiko
8 13 Ookubo Hiroshi
Please return borrowed books by the due date. If the book is returned after the due date, you may not be able to borrow another.
The due date is one month after the day you borrowed the book.
01685
A647-×

MY GRAND-FATHER GOT LOTS OF DISCARDED BOOKS FROM THE LIBRARY.
THAT'S KIND OF NEAT.

I THINK IF YOU READ IT FIRST, AND...
WERE THE FIRST TO HAVE YOUR NAME WRITTEN ON THE CARD...
WELL, IT MUST HAVE FELT NICE.

WHAT? FROM HER HOUSE?
SERIOUSLY?

WOW!
I'LL HELP!
WOW~!!

RIGHT.
ME, TOO.
SAME.

BUZZ
BUZZ

RURI!

PLEASE STOP THAT.
WHAAA?

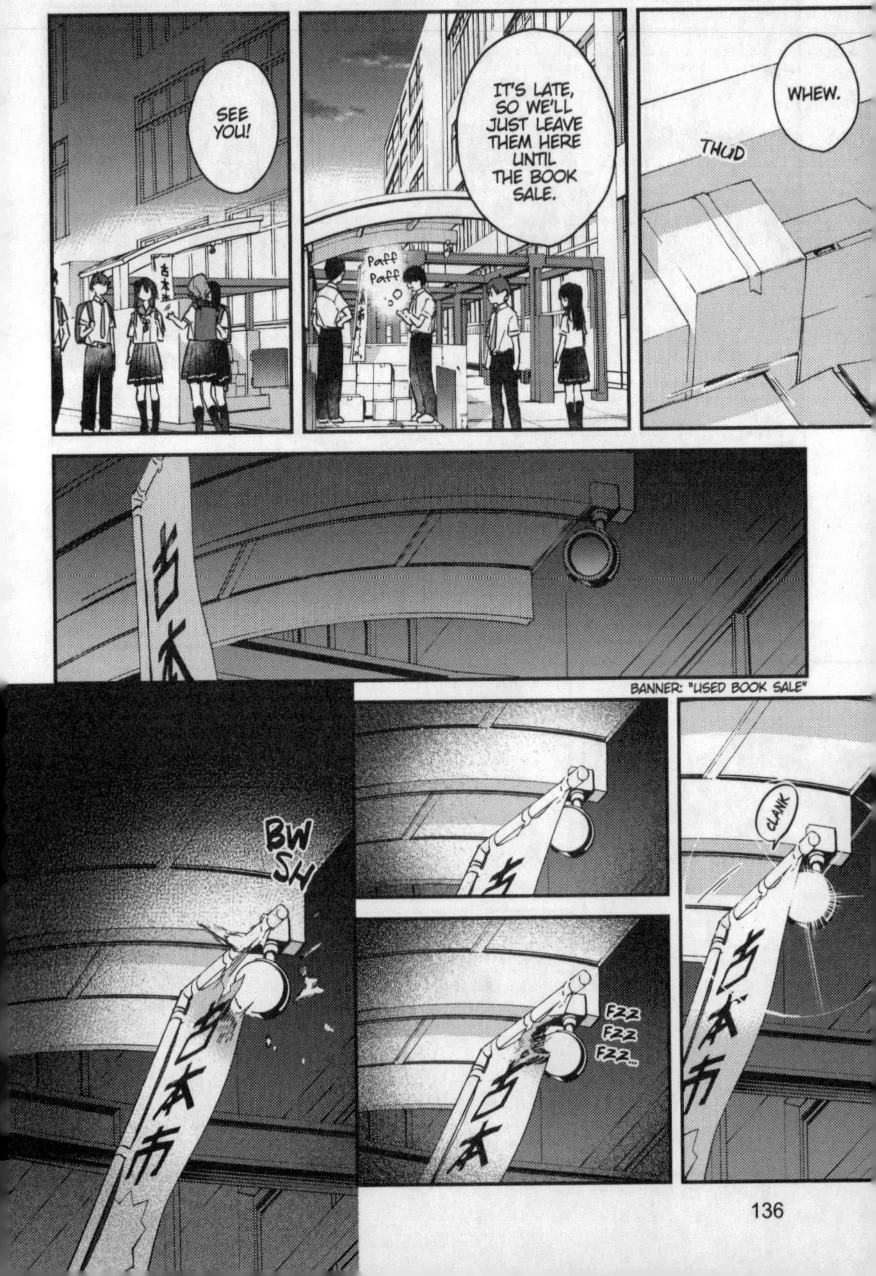

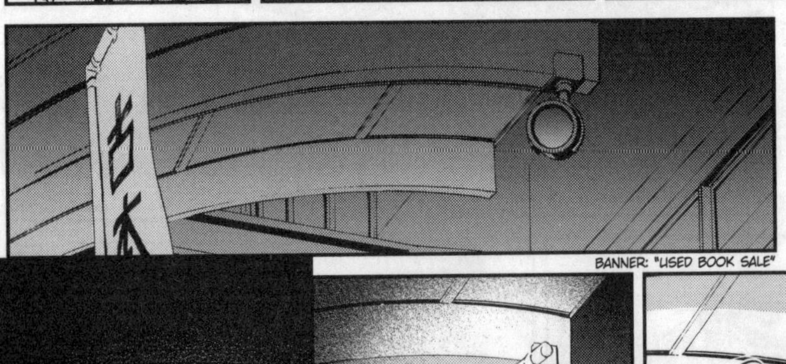

BANNER: "USED BOOK SALE"

CLANK

FZZ FZZ FZZ...

BW SH

KEEP OUT POLICE LINE
DO NOT CROSS
MURMUR
MURMUR
MURMUR
KYOTO POLICE
DO NOT CROSS
KYOTO POLICE
KEEP OUT POLICE LINE

LUCKY THE REST OF THE SCHOOL WASN'T BURNED DOWN, HUH?

THEY SAID IT WAS THE LIGHT.
THAT ONE.

IF YOU KNEW, COULDN'T YOU HAVE STOPPED IT?

THEN THE RECORD WOULD'VE CHANGED.

THAT FIRE WAS A NECESSARY EVENT.

BUT THAT'S...!
DASH

THE USED BOOK SALE HAD BEEN CANCELED.

Fzz Fzz

YOU GO DO THE SAME.

flutter
"YOU HAVE TO DO WHAT WAS RE-CORDED, OR YOU WON'T BE ABLE TO SAVE HER.
"YOU KNOW THAT."
I GUESS THAT'S TRUE.
I MEAN, IT MAKES SENSE, BUT...
BUT...
trot
trot
trot
HMPH.
LIBRARY

FLASH

NOT AGAIN!

EVEN IF I CAN PHYSICALLY MAKE BOOKS...
THE WRITING IS JUST GIBBERISH.

IT'S BECAUSE I DON'T KNOW WHAT'S INSIDE THE BOOK.
I GUESS IT REALLY IS IMPOSSIBLE.

IT'S THE FIRST TIME I EVER SAW ICHIGYOU-SAN LOOK SO SAD.

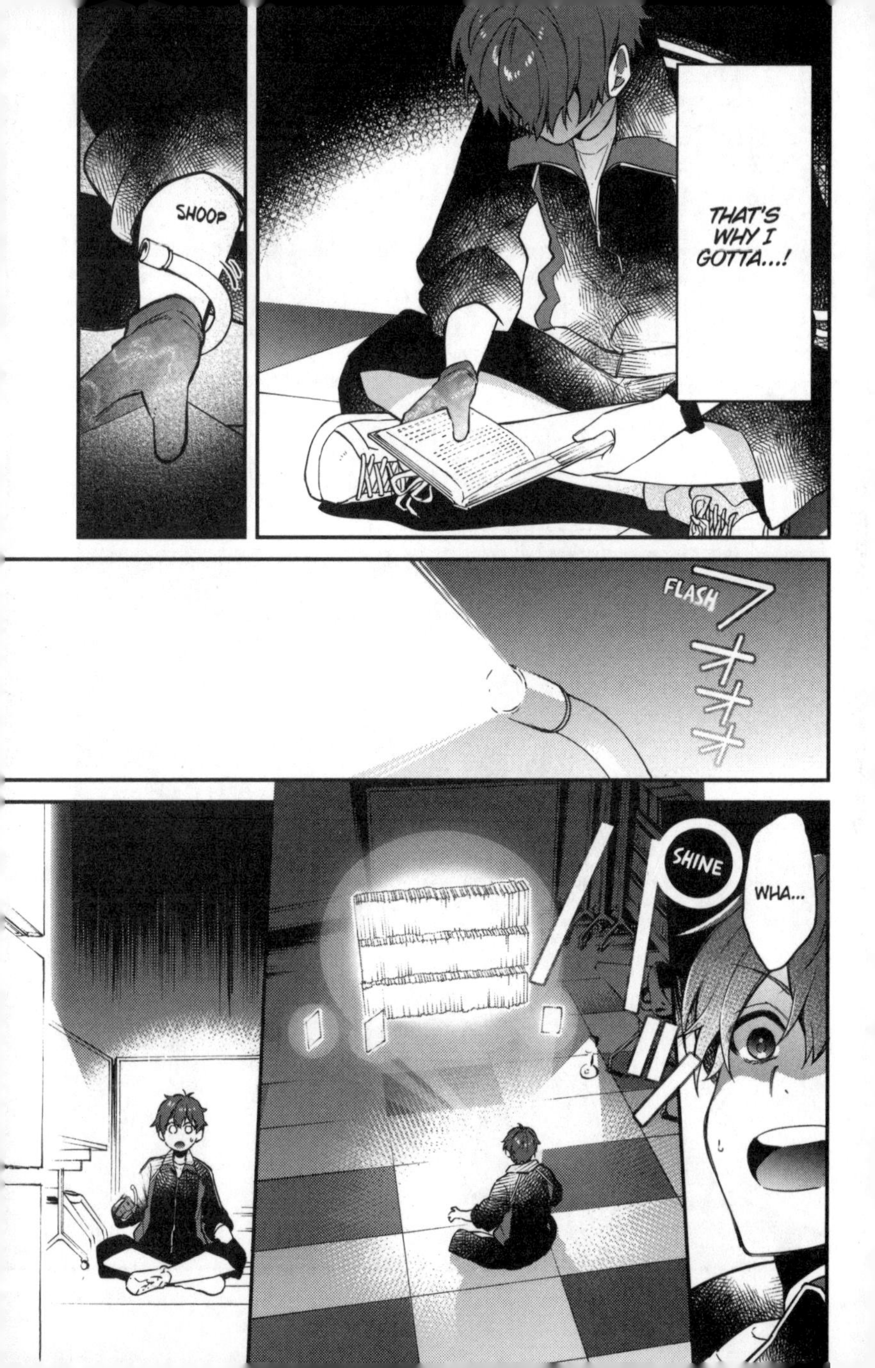

SHINE

WHA...

BLIP

......

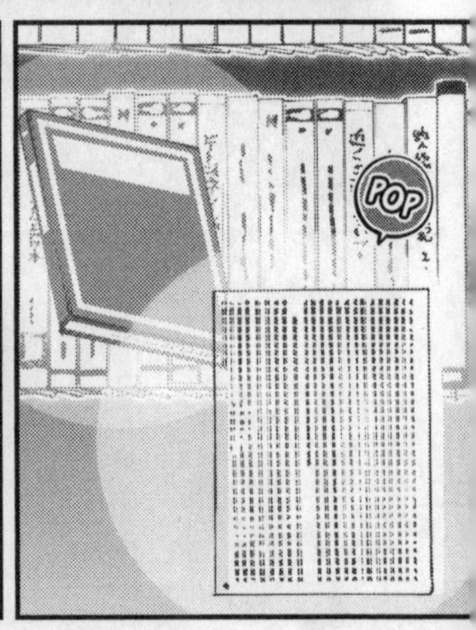

SENSEI!

THANK YOU!

SCRATCH SCRATCH

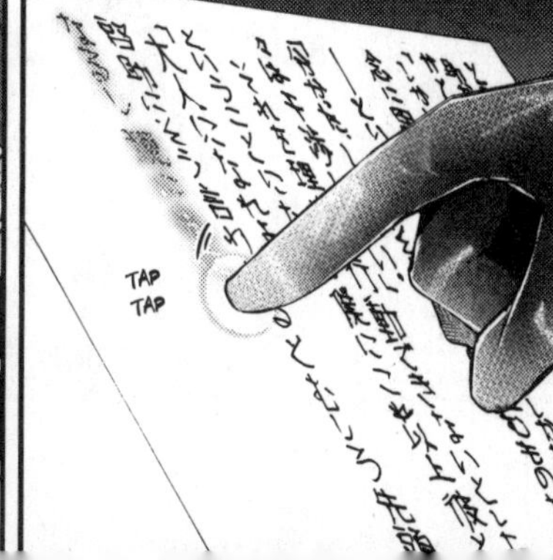
TAP TAP

Used Book Sale,
The Next Day.

GOOD MORNING.

Wobble
Wobble

UMM.
THE TRUTH IS...

THE STRANGE DEATH OF I
HOW...?
UH...
SWAY
SWAY
IT LOOKS LIKE ONE BOX WAS IN A DIFFERENT PLACE, SO THESE DIDN'T BURN IN THE FIRE.
THERE'S NOT EVEN FIFTY BOOKS HERE, BUT...
AND THIS ONE?

The City at the Bottom of the Big Lake
By Jean Matark Gabin
Translated by Masako Honchi

Flip...

GOOD THING SOME OF THE BOOKS WERE ALL RIGHT, HUH?

KATAGAKI-SAN!
DID YOU...

STUMBLE
SNORE...
ZZZ..
ZZZ..
Title The City at the Bottom of the Big Lake
Date Due
Date Returned
Borrower's Name
Date Loaned
6 25 Ichigyou Ruri
7 6 Ogiwara Yumiko
8 13 Ookubo Hiroshi
3 29 Nakayama Masami
○ Please return borrowed books by the due date. If the book is returned after the due date, you may not be able to borrow another.
○ The due date is one month after the day you borrowed the book.
01685
A647 - x

HELLO WORLD
THE MANGA

Phase5

Zzz..
Zzz..

Blink

LURCH
OH!
THE BOOK SALE!

I DIDN'T WANT TO WAKE YOU.

YOU NEEDED THE SLEEP.

I DID IT.

SLAM

ぱ

DONATED AMOUNT 34,850 YEN

SOLD OUT!!

んっ

NICE!

THANK YOU.
OH NO... I...
I HAVEN'T DONE ANY...
THAT'S RIGHT.
I DIDN'T DO ANY-THING.
TO ICHIGYOU-SAN, I JUST HAPPENED TO FIND SOME BOOKS THAT WEREN'T BURNED.
TO HER, I HAVEN'T DONE MUCH.
THANK YOU.

UH...
BA-THUMP

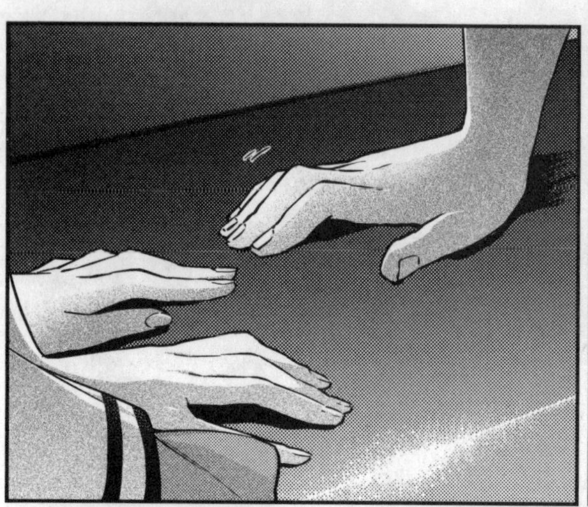

UH...
I...

?

NO...

I...LIKE YOU...
ICHIGYOU-SAN.
......!
I...I SAID IT!
WHAT'LL I DO IF SHE STARTS IGNORING ME?
I WENT OFF THE SCRIPT IN THE MANUAL!
WHAT IF THE FUTURE CHANGED BECAUSE I DID SOMETHING MYSELF?
WHAT DO I DO?!
Ba-Thud
Ba-Thud
Ba-Thud
Ba-Thud

I SEE.

GOING OUT WITH SOMEONE ISN'T SOMETHING YOU CAN DO ALONE.

SO...

SHALL WE TRY IT, THE TWO OF US?

OH, KATAGAKI-SAN, THAT BOOK YOU WANTED TO READ!
I KEPT IT FOR YOU!
UH! YES!

SLAM
Pitter patter...

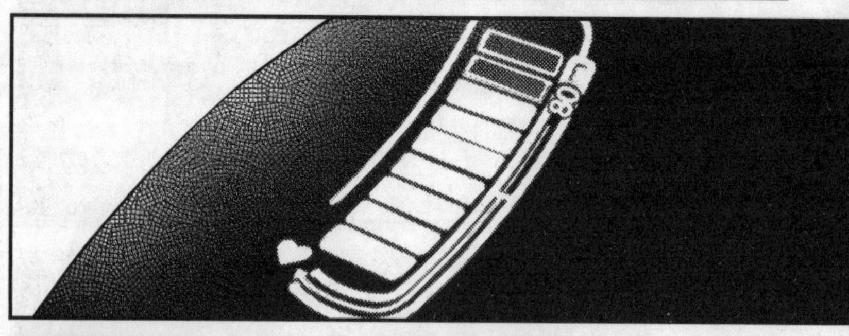
80

NEARLY THERE...

RELEASE YOUR IMAGINATION!
GWROOO

LET THE IMAGE GO WILD!
OKAY!
OOO
OOO

YOU CAN DO IT!
YOU CAN DO ANY-THING!
YOU CAN DO ANYTHING YOU PUT YOUR MIND TO!
GWOOOO
BECOME...
THE GOD OF THIS WORLD!!

FLASH
GWOOO
OOO

BUSTLE

BUSTLE

JR
Uji Station
Train Station

BUSTLE

Lantern: Ujigawa   Sign: Ujigawa Fireworks Festival, Administration Headquarters

THERE AREN'T ANY RAIN CLOUDS AROUND, SO...

IF I JUST WAIT HERE, WE CAN AVOID THE ACCIDENT, RIGHT?

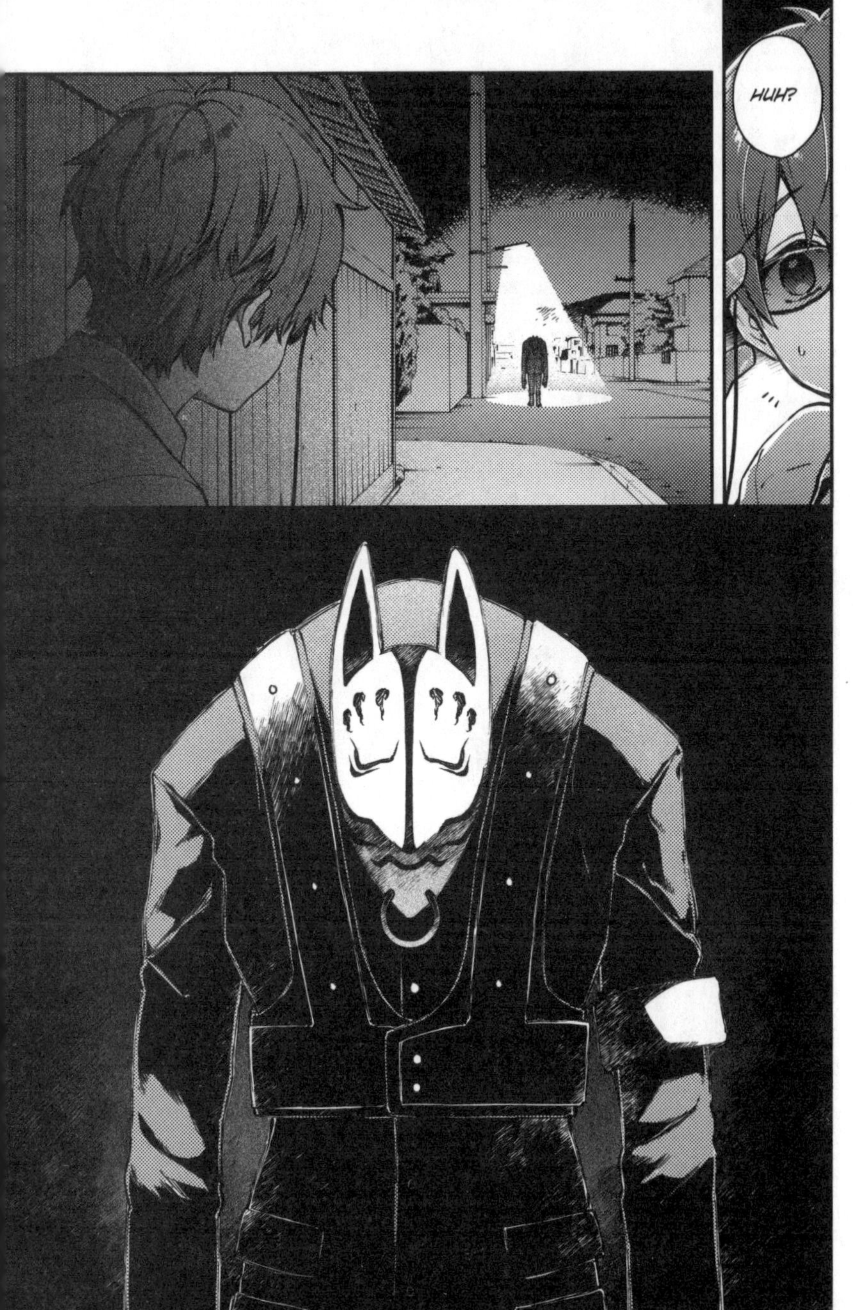
HUH?

WHAT?
SHWP
NO ONE'S THERE.
BWSH
ばっ
WH...
WHAT ARE THOSE?!
HWOO
HWOO
THAT'S...!
THE AUTOMATED REPAIR SYSTEM!
VOOM...
ALLTALE HOMEOSTATIC SYSTEM

ALLTALE NOTICED RECORDS AND FILES HAVE BEEN ALTERED, NOW THEY'RE TRYING TO CORRECT THEM!

THEY'RE GOING TO FORCE THE ACCIDENT BY TAKING BOTH OF YOU TO THE FESTIVAL, LIKE IN THE RECORDS!

Crackle
HMM?
A BOOK?
WHY DIDN'T YOU MAKE SOMETHING USEFUL?!
HUH? WHAT...
IT'S THE FIRST THING I THOUGHT OF!
THE PEN IS MIGHTIER THAN THE SWORD...
INCO-MING!
ACK!
CLANG
WHAT SHOULD I DO?!
DON'T BE AFRAID!

NNGRPH!
BYUUU
THUNK

FWOO
I DID IT!
I INTERFERED! I CAN DO THIS!
THAT'S WHAT THE GOD HAND IS FOR!
THMP
WE'LL GUARD HER UNTIL THE TIME OF THE LIGHTING STRIKE PASSES!
GOT IT?!

HOLD ON UNTIL THEN!
DASH
OKAY!!
THA-THUNK
THWAM

GOOD JOB!

FIVE MORE MINUTES! WE CAN DO THIS!

ZURRR

!

HUH?!
WHAT ARE THEY DOING NOW?!
BWOOO
WHAT?!
BWSH
BWSH
BWSH
CRAP!

NAOMI, RUN!
BWOOSH

Lantern: Ujigawa Sign: Ujigawa Fireworks Festival, Administration Headquarters

THUNDER?
BUT IT'S NOT RAINING.
CHATTER
CHATTER
VRRRSH

!!

WHA ...?
EH? HUH?!

THIS IS...

THEY'RE USING SYSTEM PRIVILEGES TO PULL STRINGS!
TAP
GWOOO
NAOMI, THEY GOT US!!

WHAT?!

YOU WERE WARPED TO WHERE THE LIGHTNING'S GOING TO STRIKE!

YOU'RE RIGHT!
I CAN SEE THE FIREWORKS FESTIVAL!

WHAT'S GOING...?

ICHIGYOU-SAN, HURRY!
WHAT?

EEK!
THWAM

TWO MORE MINUTES!

squeeze

HELLO WORLD

THE MANGA

THE ALLTALE'S RECORDS SAY ICHIGYOU-SAN WOULD BE HURT IN A FREAK ACCIDENT.
ITS AUTOMATED REPAIR SYSTEM WENT SO FAR AS TO WARP US HERE.
Phase6
THERE'S NOT MUCH TIME UNTIL THE LIGHTNING STRIKES!
THERE'S NOWHERE TO RUN EITHER.

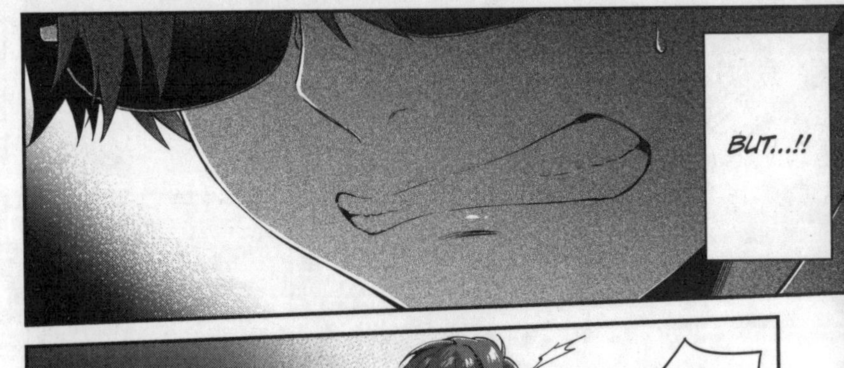

THIS IS IT!

DON'T WORRY ABOUT POSSIBLE CHANGES!!

GO FOR IT!
YES!
GHH GHH

UNGH!
OOO
OOO
GAH!
AHH!
GUH!
AHHH!
OOO

MURMUR
MURMUR
CRACKLE
BWSH
BWOO
BWOM
GRRR...
!
CRACKLE
BWSH

THEY'RE GOING TO THROW EVERYTHING AT US!

ZRR

IT'S NO USE!

NO MATTER WHAT THEY DO, THEY CAN'T STOP US!

ZRR

ZRR

EVEN IF IT'S MORE THAN A HUMAN CAN HANDLE!

THWAM

THWAM

ZRR

ZRR

EVEN IF...

BWOOSH

YOU MUST BREAK THE LAWS OF THIS WORLD!

CRACKLE
DON'T GET IN MY WAY!!
YOU CAN DO IT.
IMAGINE IT!!
The Creation of a Black Hole

FLASH

ZRR
ZRR

THWOOOM
ZRZZ
ZRZZ
ZRZZ
ZRZZ

ZRZZZ
BOOM
SHAA
SHAA

I...DID IT?!

YES!!

......?

SHUUUU

KATA-GAKI... SAN?
WHAT... WAS...?
ICHIGYOU-SAN!!
ダッ
DASH
WE DID IT!!
WE DID IT, ICHIGYOU-SAN!!
YOU'RE SAFE!!

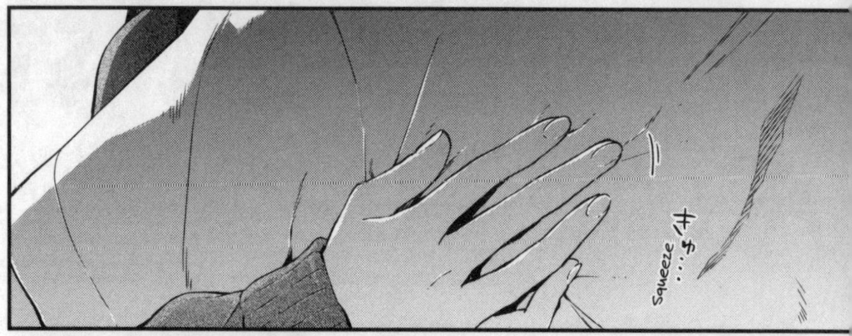
キュ…
Squeeze

ぱ!! JOLT
ACK! S-SORRY!

ERM...
I GOT CAUGHT UP IN THE MOMENT...

WHOOSH
BE-BEEP
BEEEEEEP
WHOA!
FWOOM
FLAP
FLASH

KA-KRAK

KATA-GAKI-SAN!

ICHI-GYOU-SAN!!

THIS IS...?!

THE "VESSEL" AND THE "CONTENTS" HAVE TO BE THE SAME.

WHAT?

SHE'S FALLEN IN LOVE.

BUT SHE LOVES YOU.

AND NOW....
HER MIND'S CAUGHT UP WITH THE REAL-WORLD TIMELINE.

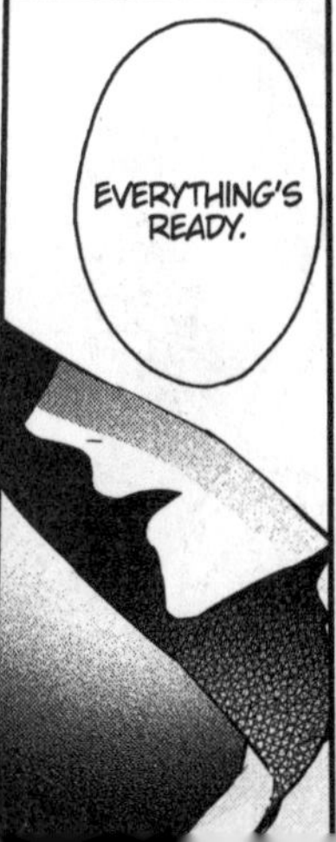
EVERYTHING'S READY.

UM?
WHAT ARE YOU TALKING ABOUT?

SHE DIDN'T DIE AFTER THE LIGHTNING STRUCK HER.

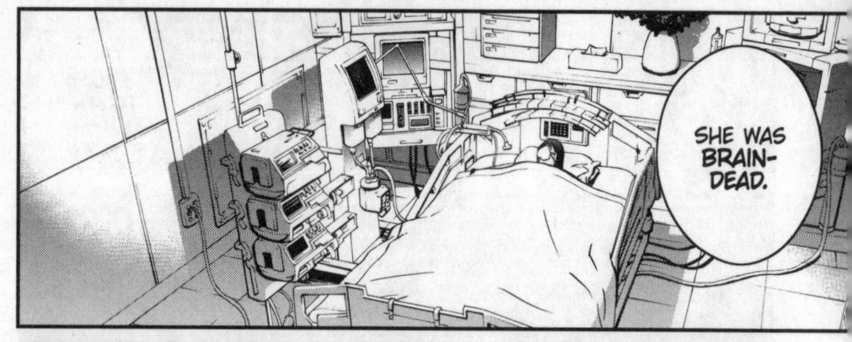

IN THE REAL WORLD SHE HAS NO CRANIAL NERVES.

I'LL REPAIR HER MIND WITH THE QUANTUM DATA FROM THE RECORDED WORLD.

I NEEDED TO FIX THE DISPARITY BETWEEN THE "REAL" HER AND THE "RECORDED" HER.

THE MEASURED VALUE IS GREATER THAN THE SENSORY THRESHOLD.
EH?!
...?!
BUT I CAN "ALIGN" THEM.
Float

AAAHHHH!
HELP!
STOOOOOP!!

GOODBYE...
NAOMI.

DRIP
SHAAAA

ICHI-GYOU...
SHAAAAAAAA
OH.
I'LL BRING ICHIGYOU-SAN BACK USING...!
UM!
MAYBE SHE'S AT HOME?

DASH

WHAT IS...
THIS?

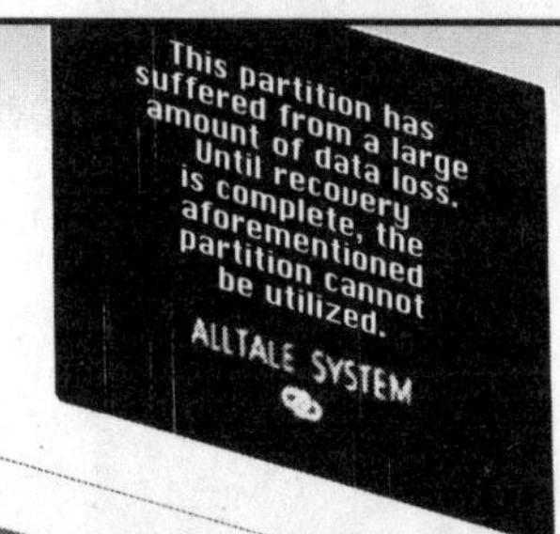
This partition has suffered from a large amount of data loss. Until recovery is complete, the aforementioned partition cannot be utilized.
ALLTALE SYSTEM

OPEN UP!
BAM
FLAIL
OPEN UP!!
GIVE ICHIGYOU-SAN BACK!
BAM
BAM
BAM
ICHIGYOU-SAN!!
SHAAAAA
SHAAAA

BEEP ピッ
BEEP ピッ
BEEP ピッ
BEEP ピッ

BEEP ピッ

ICHI-GYOU-SAN.

......

I'VE WAITED SO LONG.

2037, Kyoto.

HELLO WORLD
THE MANGA

CLOMP
CLOMP
CLOMP
Phase 7

AMENTIA, PROGRESSING.

THE PARTITIONS ARE EXPANDING!

Beep

Beep

Beep

THE INDEPENDENT RECORDS MODULES...

CAN'T BE MADE ANY LARGER!

SENKO-SAN.
SHUU-SAN.
Clomp
Clomp

NAOMI!

ALLTALE EXPERIENCED AN ERROR AND SOME OF THE RECORDS WERE DAMAGED.
WE HAVEN'T IDENTIFIED THE CAUSE.

ANY IDEAS?

NO.
REGARDLESS OF *HOW* IT HAPPENED, WE HAVE A BIGGER PROBLEM NOW.

THE AREAS CAUSING THE CHANGES ARE INFECTING OTHER RECORDS.

AT THIS RATE, THE BUTTERFLY EFFECT WILL SURPASS THE THRESHOLD.

WE'RE TALKING CHAIN DECAY.
NOT GOOD.

AIEE.
WELL ...
WE BETTER FIX THIS.

WHAT DO WE DO?

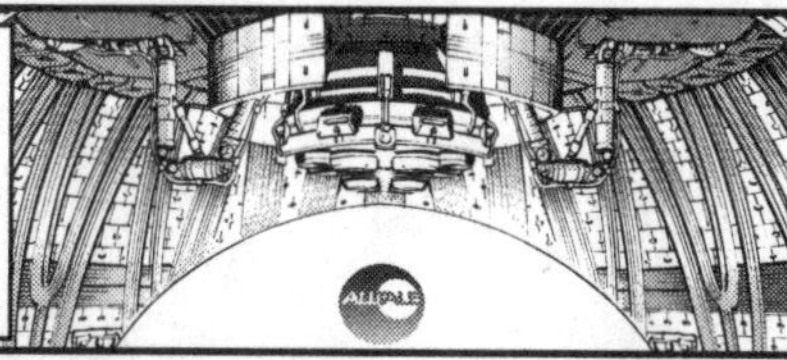

CHATTER

WE MUST SAVE THE HARD DRIVE!

WE'LL BLOCK THE RECORDS AND RETRIEVE THEM!

THEN WE CAN WORRY ABOUT RECOVERY!

THIS IS SERIOUS!

CAN YOU GET ON IT RIGHT AWAY?

YES.

I'LL GO CHANGE.
CLOMP CLOMP

I'm totally used to it now so...

I'll be done before I know it.

When I do it by myself...
ICHIGYOU-SAN HASN'T WOKEN UP SINCE THE LIGHTNING INCIDENT.
I KEPT VISITING HER AT THE HOSPITAL ANYWAY.
TIME PASSED. I MOVED THROUGH LIFE AIM-LESSLY.
THEN I TOOK A COLLEGE CLASS THAT CHANGED EVERY-THING.

he Possibilities
of Quantum Records
Using quantum
of the brain
Senko Tsunehisa

PROFESSOR SENKO, A KEY FIGURE IN THE ALLTALE PROJECT, HAD A THEORY.

The Possibilities
of Quantum Records
Using quantum data of the brain
Senko Tsunehisa

I KNEW THEN WHAT I MUST DO.

QUANTUM RECORD TECHNOLOGY. THE KYOTO RECORD PROJECT.

THE **ALLTALE.**

OF COURSE, I'D NEED EXTENSIVE KNOWLEDGE AND ACADEMIC ACHIEVEMENTS.

I SACRIFICED **EVERYTHING** TO GET HERE.

FINALLY, I HAD IT IN MY HANDS.
BEEP
SWOOSH
THE KEY TO...
MY PLAN.

CREAK
TAP

ZA-SNAP
!
WHA?!
BWSH
UGH.
SHUUU...
HUFF!
HUFF!
FLUTTER
IT DIDN'T WORK ON THE FIRST TRY.
BUT MY THEORY WAS CORRECT.
WITH THIS...
I WAS ABLE TO GET "IN."

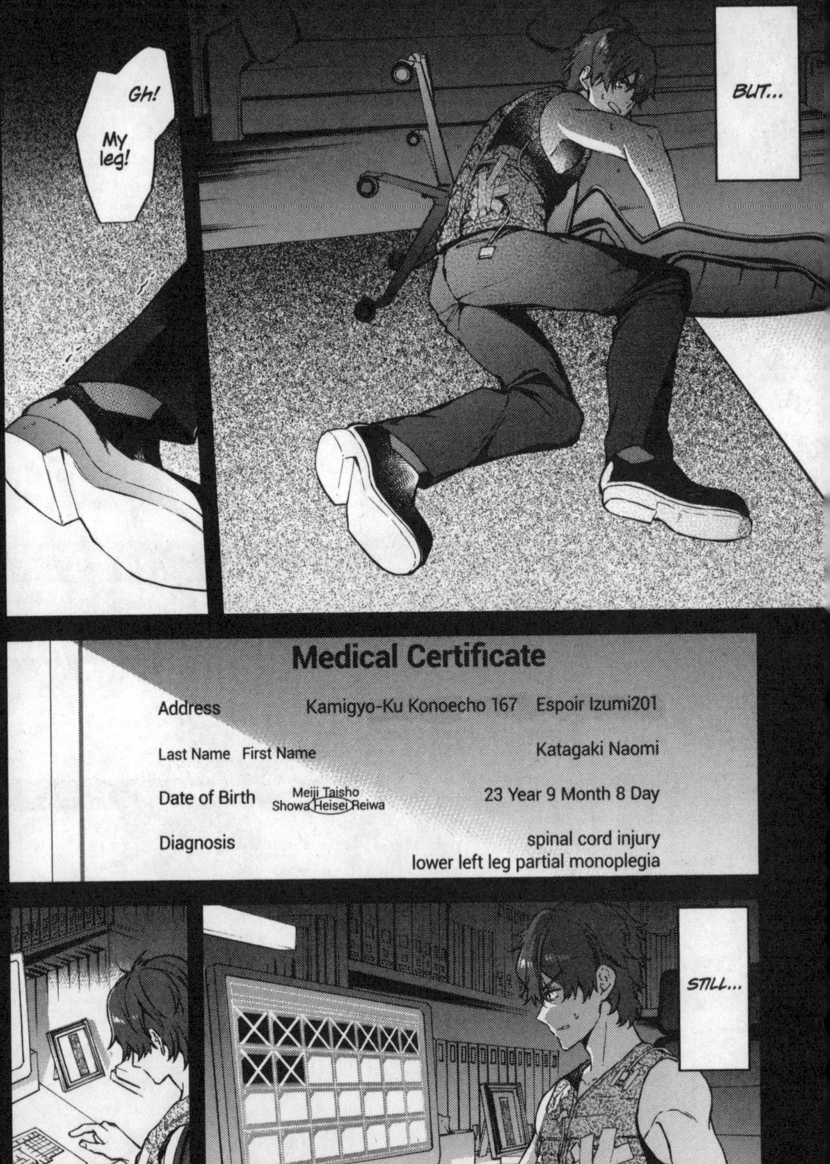

BUT...

Gh!

My leg!

Medical Certificate

Address	Kamigyo-Ku Konoecho 167 Espoir Izumi201
Last Name First Name	Katagaki Naomi
Date of Birth Meiji Taisho Showa Heisei Reiwa	23 Year 9 Month 8 Day
Diagnosis	spinal cord injury lower left leg partial monoplegia

IF I COULD SEE YOU AGAIN, THEN...!!

BECAUSE THE PRECISE SURVEY WOULD AFFECT THE ORIGINAL DATA.

QUANTUM MIND DATA CAN'T BE COPIED...

THMP

THAT'S ALL I DID...

I GUESS THERE'S NOTHING ELSE TO BE DONE.

STAND BY
RECOVERY
BEEP

RECOVERY WILL BE COMPLETE IN APPROXIMATELY EIGHTY HOURS.
BUT RESTORATION WILL TAKE NEARLY A DECADE.

NAOMI?
YEAH.

RUN SYSTEM RECOVERY?
YES
NO

IF I DO THIS, THE RECORDED WORLD WILL DIS-APPEAR.

SO WILL EVERYONE INSIDE IT.

AND THEN...

BEEP

BEEP
ATC
HMC
RECOVERY
ACCEPTED
YAAAY!

IT WAS ALL JUST DATA.
THAT'S ALL.

IT'S THE RIGHT THING TO DO.

RATTLE

I KNOW IT'S ALL A LOT TO TAKE IN.

AFTER THE LIGHTNING STRUCK, YOU WERE IN A COMA. IT'S A MIRACLE YOU WOKE UP.

IN THOSE TEN YEARS...
A LOT HAPPENED.
Creak
I GOT IN AN ACCIDENT, TOO.
I'M SO HAPPY YOU'RE AWAKE.
I'M GLAD I DIDN'T GIVE UP.
DO YOU REMEM-BER?
THAT DAY, THE FIREWORKS FESTIVAL?

HERE...

Squeeze...
I'VE BEEN WAITING...
THIS WHOLE TIME.

THAT BOOK.
……
WHAT?
PRESS
CREAK…
NOT THE SAME.

YOU'RE...
NOT KATAGAKI-SAN!

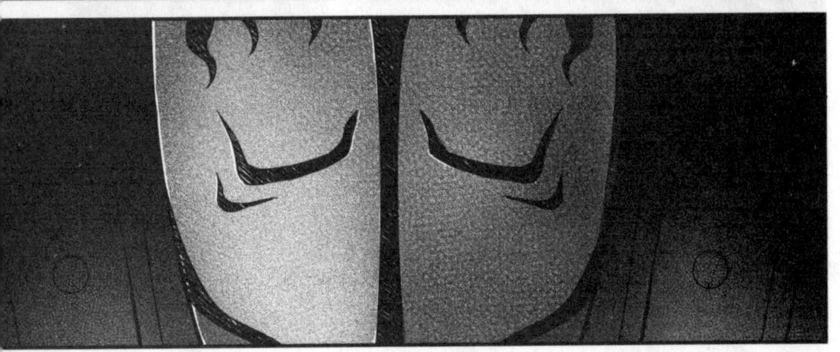

HUH?!
CLATTER
WHAT?
THE ALLTALE AUTOMATED REPAIR SYSTEM?!
blam
WHY ARE THEY HERE?!
WHAM

BAM
BAM
BAM
BAM
IF THEY'RE HERE, THAT MEANS...!
N-NO!
ME AND...
NO.
THIS WORLD'S ...
INSIDE THE ALLTALE?!

BAM
BAM
BAM
BAM

HELLO WORLD
THE MANGA

Phase8
BAM
THUD
NGH!
SQUEEZE...

IF THIS IS ALLTALE'S AUTOMATED REPAIR SYSTEM...
AND I CAN INTERACT WITH THEM...
THEN THIS WORLD, ME...
IT'S ALL DATA!
EEK!
SQUEEZE
SQUEEZE
ICHIGYOU-SAN!
RUN! GET AWAY FROM HERE!
THEY EXIST TO RESOLVE INCONSIS-TENCES IN THE RECORDS.
LIKE QUANTUM MIND DATA THAT WAS SALVAGED.
IF THE SYSTEM DECIDES SOME-THING IS A "FOREIGN OBJECT," THEN...

IT'LL BE ERASED.

AH!

AAAHH!

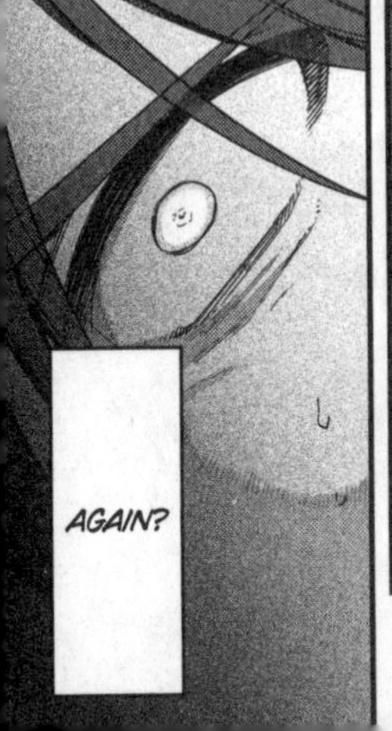

RIGHT BEFORE MY EYES, AGAIN?!
AHHHHHH!
FLASH
SLAM

WHAM
BAM
BAM
BAM
BAM
......?!
HACK!
COUGH!

KATAGAKI-SAN?
NO! HOW...?!
YOU AND THE WORLD WENT THROUGH RECOVERY...!
SHIING

SHIIING

NAOMI'S...
MEMORIES?!
VRRRR

VRRR
ALLTALE WORLD RECORD, POST-RECOVERY.
ZRR
ZRR
ZRR

ooo
ooo
ooo
That red aurora...
everything it touches disintegrates!
At this rate...
I'll also...

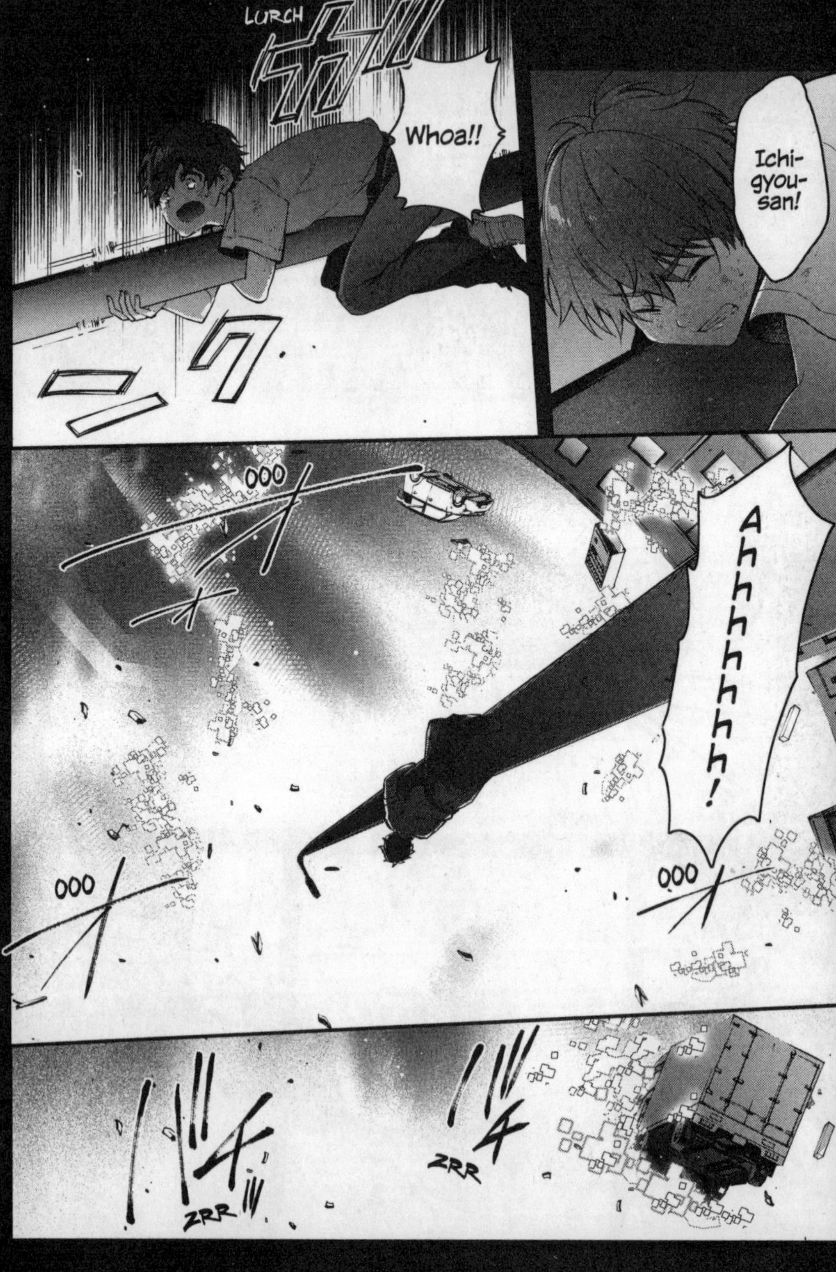
Ichi-gyou-san!
LURCH
Whoa!!
Ahhhhhhhh!
OOO
OOO
OOO
ZRR
ZRR

!
That gap...
ZRR
The things that fall in there aren't disintegrating.
ZRR
ZRR
...!
It was the same when that crow appeared.
And when Ichigyou-san was taken!

Beyond that gap...
is another world?
SIZZLE
ZRR
ZRR
Ungh.
It's such a narrow gap.
ZRR
SHAKE
SHAKE
There's...
no guarantee it leads to another world.

This always happens!

CLENCH

I freeze up and can't do anything!

I can't change even when I want to.

The Power of Decision

Start Using it Tomorrow! Practical Training

by Yuu Kumazawa

That's why...

I figured if I could change Ichigyou-san's fate...

But...
You just have to do what's written down about the future in this!
Logical Air
Ultimate Manual
MONTH 4 DAY 20 (TUESDAY)
SCHOOL IS OVER AT ABOUT 16:00
AND AT THE BUS STOP ON THE SCHOOL SIDE.
BORROW A MAGAZINE THAT ONLY THE NORTH LIBRARY CARRIES.
MONTH 4 DAY 20 (WEDNESDAY)
LIBRARY MEETING
GIVE BOOKMARK.
MAKE UP WITH RURI.
I just did what he told me to do.
I'm not a protagonist.
Safe!
I could never do anything.
But now...

Katagaki-san!

The City at the Bottom of the Big Lake
By Jean Matark Gabin
Translated by Masako Honchi

Even if it's different from the records...
even if they stop me...
I decided this by myself.
THE STRANGE DEATH OF I
That's right.
I can do it...
for you.
GRIP

BWSH
Aaaaaahhhhhh!

This is...?
Am I...
dead?
No.

You must fix it.

You must retrieve Ichigyou Ruri!

Ah!

You're ...
The God Hand?
I'm just a crow.

A crow that...
knows how much you practiced...
and built yourself up.
Katagiri Naomi-san.
Do you want to help her?

Yes!!
FLAP
GYUU

GYUUU
FLASH

JUST NOW...

NAOMI'S AND MY MEMO-RIES...
GOT MIXED TOGETH-ER?
WHAT HAPPEN-ED?

THOSE KITSUNE MASKS ARE AFTER YOU, ICHIGYOU-SAN.

ME?
WH- WHY?
I'LL EXPLAIN LATER.
IT'S ALL RIGHT.
I'M HERE TO HELP YOU.
WILL YOU LET ME?
FL-AP

BLAM
THUD

TMP
LET'S GO HOME.
LET'S GO BACK TO WHERE WE BELONG.

I WASN'T AN AVATAR.

IT WAS A VERSION OF REALITY.
I DON'T UNDERSTAND THE THEORY, BUT...

THE EXISTENCE OF TWO OF ME IN THE SAME WORLD CONFUSED THE DATA...
NO. WHO CARES ABOUT *THAT*?

I KNOW BECAUSE I SAW HIS MEMORIES.

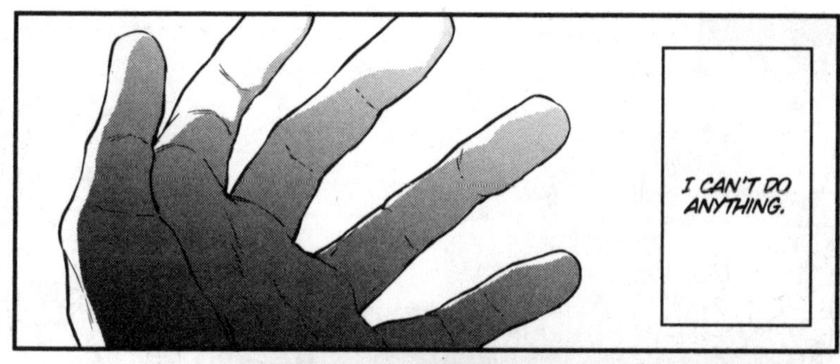

BUT...

HE MIGHT BE ABLE TO.

IT'S NECESSARY TO CONVERT ICHIGYOU RURI BACK TO THE ALLTALE AGAIN.
TROT TROT
WE NEED TO INSTALL THE QUANTUM CONVERSION APPARATUS...

WE NEED TO GO...
TO THE STAIRS OF...
KYOTO STATION!

HELLO WORLD

THE MANGA

BEEP

BEEP

ALLTALE'S QUANTUM RECORD IS LOOPING!

I'M GETTING INVALID OPERATION ERRORS!

Phase9

ALLTALE

THE REPAIR SYSTEM IS TRYING TO STOP THE INCREASE OF INFORMATION.

I DON'T UNDERSTAND WHY THAT WOULD RESULT IN SUCH PHYSICAL PHENOMENA.
THAT'S RIGHT.

ALLTALE HAS SURPASSED THE BOUNDARIES OF LOGIC AND IS INTERFERING WITH OUR WORLD.

BUT THAT MEANS SOMETHING HOMOGENOUS EXISTS HERE *AND* WITHIN ALLTALE!
WELL...

UNLESS WE STOP THOSE KITSUNE MASKS, THERE'S NO WAY WE CAN VERIFY ANYTHING.

WE CAN'T EXECUTE ORDERS FROM OUTSIDE.
ALL WE CAN DO IS CUT IT OFF DIRECTLY.

THAT'S WHAT I WAS AFRAID OF.

WHAM

WHAM

WHOOSH

DASH

DASH

DASH

DASH

IT'S LIKE
IT NEVER
ENDS...!

EEEK!
NO!

GRAB
WHOA!

VWSH
GET IN!
BWAM
DASH
SCREEEEECH
THUD
EEK!

WHY...?!
I'M TAKING HER BACK TO THE OLD WORLD!
THIS IS ALL MY FAULT.
I NEVER WANTED THIS TO HAPPEN.
I DIDN'T MEAN FOR YOU TO SUFFER LIKE THIS.
I...
JUST WANTED TO SEE HER SMILE AGAIN.

"I JUST WANT HER SMILING AND HAPPY...

"EVEN IF IT ISN'T REAL."

I'LL MAKE IT UP TO YOU.

WHERE SHOULD I GO?
NAOMI, ORDERS, PLEASE.

THOSE BIG STAIRS AT KYOTO STATION.

CON-VERTER.

BWO

SHUU

THUD

THUD

WHOA!

EEK!

THUD

SHUUU
FLASH
I'LL MAKE A GATE.
AS YOU STEP THROUGH, ICHIGYOU RURI'S QUANTUM CONVER- SION WILL BE PRO- CESSED.
BY DESCENDING THE STAIRS, YOU'LL RETURN TO YOUR PREVIOUS WORLD.

THERE'S NO TIME.

THE GOD HAND...
YOU...

STEP CONVERSION?
THAT MEANS...

THIS AREA IS UNDER SYSTEM CONTROL AND IT'S GROWING.

ICHIGYOU RURI MUST CONVERT! THEN, KATAGAKI NAOMI-SAN.

AH!

THAT'S IMPOSSIBLE.

SHE WAS BEDRIDDEN AND...
HAS A FEAR OF HEIGHTS.

TO GO DOWN THERE, WITH HER LEGS SO WEAK, IT'S TOO MUCH!

I HAVE TO DO SOMETHING.
ICHI...
ICHIGYOU-SAN.

IT'S OKAY.

LET'S DO IT!
OKAY.

I SEE.

THESE TWO HAVE EACH OTHER.

SHE'S NOT THE SAME GIRL, PARALYZED WITH FEAR.

WOBBLE

THEY'RE NOW A UNITED PAIR...
WHO CAN OVERCOME ANYTHING.

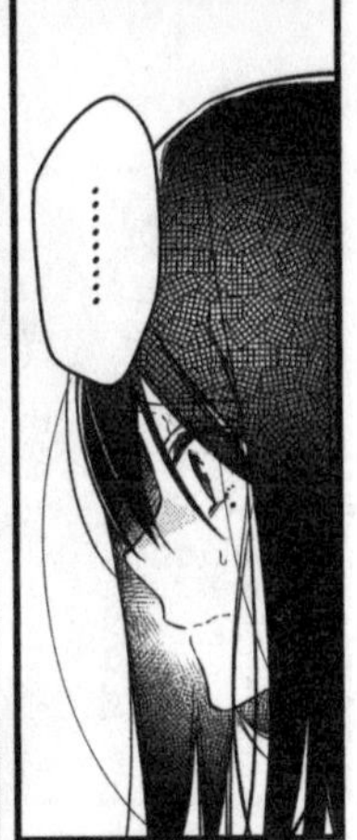
......

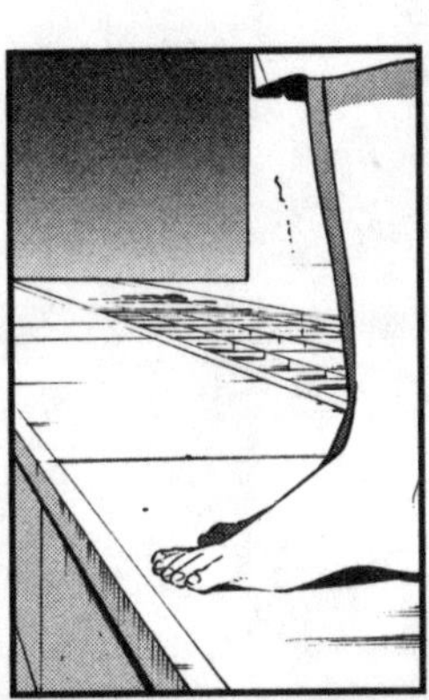

HURRY.
GO!

WHAT'S WRONG?

ARE YOU...
KATAGAKI-SAN?
NO.
HE'S KATAGAKI NAOMI.

I'M JUST AN EXTRA.

THAT'S RIGHT.

HE PROTECTS THE HEROINE.
HE'S THE STORY'S PROTAGONIST.

NOW ...

YOU LOVED ME, DIDN'T YOU?

THANK YOU.

GOODBYE.
FLOAT
TAP

SHING
TAP...
ICHI-
GYOU-
SAN.

EVEN THOUGH I WAS INDECISIVE AND TIMID... I MANAGED TO OVERCOME ALL THAT AND CHOSE HER.

WHEN ICHIGYOU-SAN FELL INTO A COMA...

I LOST MY FUTURE.

I DECIDED TO DO WHATEVER IT TOOK TO GET HER BACK.

I DECIDED TO TAKE BACK OUR FUTURE.
ICHI-GYOU-SAN...
I...

I...
LOVED YOU SO MUCH.

OKAY!
IT'S YOUR TURN NEXT.
PLEASE HURRY, THIS AREA IS ABOUT TO BE CONSUMED.
ALL RIGHT! HERE I GO!
DASH

WATCH OUT!!

KA-WHOOM
WHOA!!
CLATTER

オォ
OOO
オ

ROAR
GAAAHH!
WHOA!!
GRIK
GRIK
GRIIIK
KRIK
CRACK
KRIK

ROAAAR
NNNGH!
GRIK
GRIK
INSTEAD OF USING NUMBERS TO OVERWHELM US...
THEY'RE GOING WITH A MASSIVE SHOW OF FORCE!
GRIK
...!

ROAAAR
SENSEI!
I CAN'T...!
GRIIK
NAOMI!
Y-YEAH?!
THERE'S A WAY TO DEFEAT IT!

TELL ME!
WHAT SHOULD I DO?!
USE THE GOD HAND...
TO ERASE ME.

HELLO WORLD

THE MANGA

SHOVE

NNNNGH!

SHOVE

SHOVE

Phase 10

WE WON'T BE ABLE TO CONTROL IT AND THE DATA WILL INCREASE INFINITELY!
AllTale
Automated Repair System
THE AUTOMATED REPAIR SYSTEM IS ALLTALE'S CONTROL ROD!
IT KEEPS THE RECORD OUTPUT TO A BARE MINIMUM SO THE ALLTALE CAN OPERATE!
IF YOU STOP IT THEN...
YES!
IT'S JUST LIKE THE BIG BANG!
IN JAPA-NESE...
IT'S CALLED "KAIBYAKU"! CREATION!
IN SHORT, IF YOU STOP THIS, IN RETURN FOR THE KITSUNE MASKS STOPPING...

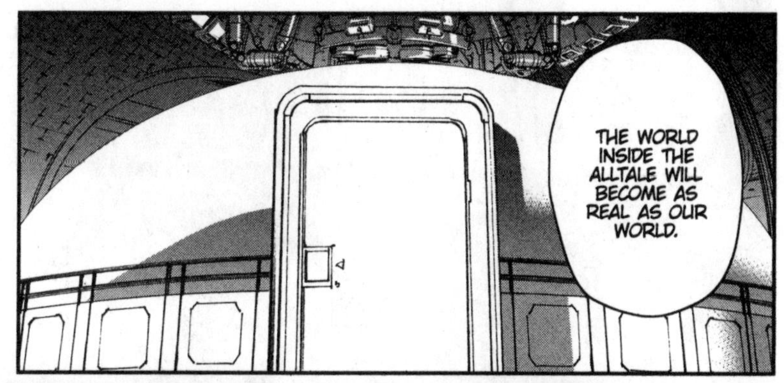

ROAR

ROAR

ROAR

ROAR

ERASE YOU?!

YOU GET IT, RIGHT?
THERE'S NO GUARANTEE THOSE KITSUNE MASKS WILL DISAPPEAR!
THEY WERE TRYING TO ERASE ICHIGYOU-SAN BECAUSE HER "CONSCIOUSNESS" AND "PHYSICAL BODY" WERE DIFFERENT.
Consciousness (2027)
Physical body (2037)
NOW THAT SHE'S RETURNED...
IT WANTS ONE OF US.
IF ONE OF US DISAPPEARS FROM THIS WORLD, THEN THEY'LL STOP.
THE WORLD CAN'T DEAL WITH TWO OF US.
IT'S THE ONLY WAY OUT!
I CAN'T!!

IT'S OKAY! WE CAN DO THIS!
I'LL JUST DEFEAT THIS ONE!
THEN WE'LL MAKE ANOTHER CONVERSION APPARATUS ...!
CLANK
GA
NO, I TRICKED YOU!
I USED YOU!
DON'T HESITATE! END ME!
I DON'T WANT TO.
....

WE...
WE'RE THE SAME!
I SAW THEM!
I SAW YOUR MEMORIES, SENSEI!
I'M THE SAME AS YOU!
NO MATTER HOW HARD IT GOT!
EVEN IF IT RUINED MY LEG!
IF THAT'S WHAT IT TOOK TO SAVE HER...
I WOULD HAVE DONE THE SAME THING!
YOU DID ALL THAT AND...
YOU GOT NOTHING!
I CAN'T ACCEPT THAT!

JUST BELIEVE!
THEN YOU CAN DO ANYTHING!
THAT'S WHAT YOU SAID, SENSEI!
JUST DO IT!
LIVE!
WHIRL
CLANK
CLANK
BOTH OF US WILL!
WHOOSH

THUD

SHUUUU
AH...
AH...!

SHUUUU
IF YOU BELIEVE, YOU CAN DO ANYTHING.
THAT'S RIGHT.
EVEN MY LEG, THAT'S NOT SUPPOSED TO BE WEAK...
SEE...?

SENSEI!

YOU LOOKED COOL, YOU KNOW...
LIKE A PROTAG-ONIST.

YOU...
LIVE YOUR STORY.

YOU'RE THE MAIN CHARACTER.
SENSEI...
SENSEI!
THERE'S NOTHING LEFT FOR ME TO TEACH YOU.

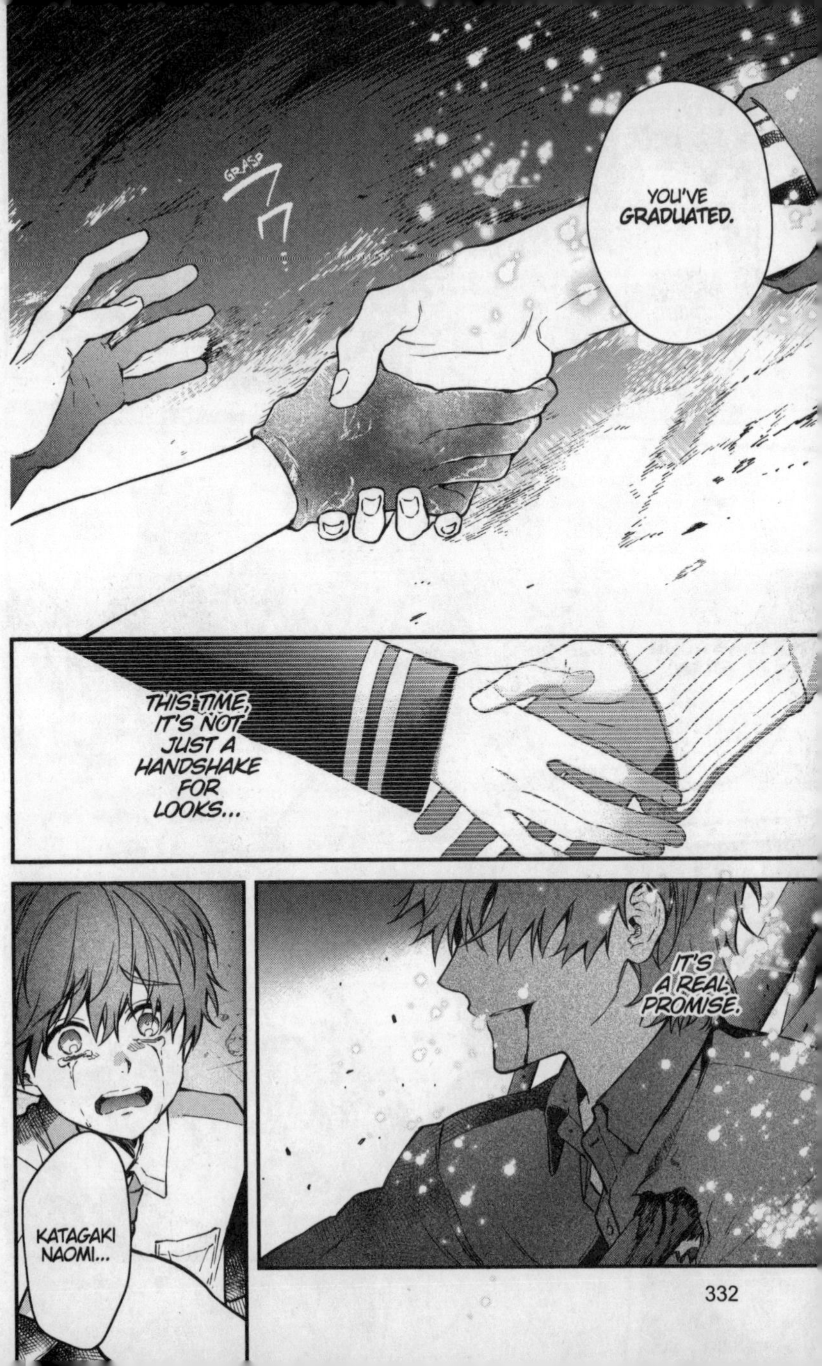

YOU'VE GRADUATED.

GRASP

THIS TIME, IT'S NOT JUST A HANDSHAKE FOR LOOKS...

BE HAPPY!

AAHHHHHHH!

YES.
THE GIRL I LOVED MOST IN THE WORLD AND...
YOU, WHO HELPED ME CHANGE.

KNOWING I CONNECTED YOUR FUTURES...
MEANS I CAN DIE HAPPY.

FREEZE
THEY STOPPED?!
TAKE THIS!!
CLUNK
1
2
3

FLASH
BWA-SHUUU
OOO
OOO

SENSEI?
ICHIGYOU-SAN?
LogicalAir
Ultimate Manual

IT'S
BLANK!

KATAGAKI-SAN.

I WONDER WHERE ALLTALE WENT?

MAYBE INTO A NEW UNIVERSE?

I DON'T KNOW WHERE, BUT...

I HOPE IT'S A KINDER UNIVERSE THAN HERE!

ARE WE BACK...
IN THE WORLD WE CAME FROM?

NO.
I BET
THIS IS...

SOMEWHERE NO ONE KNOWS ABOUT.

IT'S A NEW WORLD.

THE "VESSEL" AND "CONTENTS" NEEDED TO MATCH.

HMM?
WHAT?
WHAT IS IT THAT I HEAR?
YOU SCARIFICED EVERYTHING FOR SOMEONE WHO WAS IMPORTANT TO YOU.
YOUR GODS...
HAVE COME INTO ALIGNMENT WITH THE "VESSEL."
WHAT DOES THAT MEAN...?

WE DID IT!
YAAAY!
AAH!
WE DID IT!
IT FINALLY WORKED...?

KATAGAKI-SAN?
......
ICHIGYOU-SAN?
International Record Organization, Moon Research Lab.

The One
HELLO WORLD END

HELLO WORLD

THE MANGA

EN SEAS ENTERTAINMENT PRESENTS

ELLO WORLD

THE MANGA

Manga by **MANATSU SUZUKI** and **YOSHIHIRO SONO**
Original Concept: **"HELLO WORLD" PRODUCTION COMMITTEE**

TRANSLATION
Beni Axia Conrad

ADAPTATION
Asha Bardon

LETTERING AND RETOUCH
Carl Vanstiphout

COVER DESIGN
Hanase Qi

PROOFREADER
na Guggenheim, Dawn Davis

EDITOR
Shannon Fay

PREPRESS TECHNICIAN
nnon Rasmussen-Silverstein

PRODUCTION MANAGER
Lissa Pattillo

MANAGING EDITOR
Julie Davis

ASSOCIATE PUBLISHER
Adam Arnold

PUBLISHER
Jason DeAngelis

HELLO WORLD: The Manga
© 2019 by Manatsu Suzuki, Yoshihiro Sono
© "HELLO WORLD" Film Partners
All rights reserved.
First published in Japan in 2019 by SHUEISHA Inc., Tokyo.
English edition published by arrangement with Shueisha Inc., Tokyo in care of Tohan Corporation, Tokyo.

No portion of this book may be reproduced or transmitted in any form without written permission from the copyright holders. This is a work of fiction. Names, characters, places, and incidents are the products of the author's imagination or are used fictitiously. Any resemblance to actual events, locales, or persons, living or dead, is entirely coincidental.

Seven Seas press and purchase enquiries can be sent to Marketing Manager Lianne Sentar at press@gomanga.com. Information regarding the distribution and purchase of digital editions is available from Digital Manager CK Russell at digital@gomanga.com.

Seven Seas and the Seven Seas logo are trademarks of Seven Seas Entertainment. All rights reserved.

ISBN: 978-1-64827-591-3
Printed in Canada
First Printing: September 2021
10 9 8 7 6 5 4 3 2 1

FOLLOW US ONLINE: ***www.sevenseasentertainment.com***

READING DIRECTIONS

This book reads from ***right to left***, Japanese style. If this is your first time reading manga, you start reading from the top right panel on each page and take it from there. If you get lost, just follow the numbered diagram here. It may seem backwards at first, but you'll get the hang of it! Have fun!!

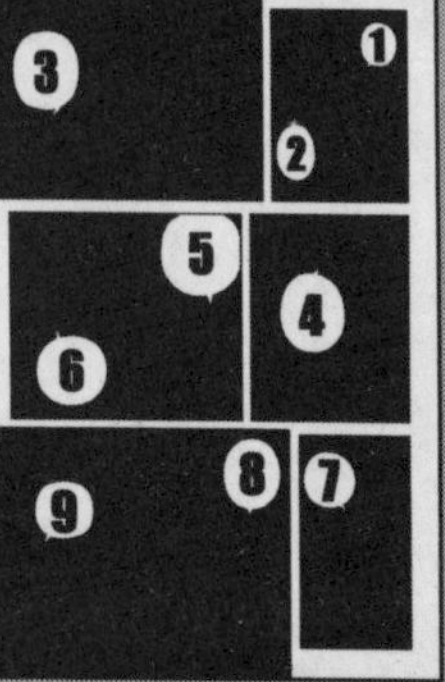